Credit Repair

Special Edition – Two Books

Learn How To Repair and Improve Your Credit
Report Quickly Using Federal Laws That Are
Designed To Protect You From Collectors,
Credit Bureaus and Banks.

Real Dispute Letters and Templates Included

Revised and Updated

Credit Repair

Special Edition – Two Books in One.

Copyright 2019 – Dana Lee

All Rights Reserved.

Published by:

CyberLearners

Cleveland, Ohio

Disclaimer:

This book is not giving any legal advice and we are not attorneys – any examples or strategies written here are the author's personal experience and opinion.

This book is reproduced below with the goal of providing information that is as accurate and reliable as possible. Regardless, purchasing this Book can be seen as consent to the fact that both the publisher and the author of this book are in no way experts on the topics discussed within and that any recommendations or suggestions that are made herein are for entertainment purposes only. Professionals should be consulted as needed prior to undertaking any of the action endorsed herein.

This declaration is deemed fair and valid by both the American Bar Association and the Committee of Publishers Association and is legally binding throughout the United States.

Furthermore, the transmission, duplication or reproduction of any of the following work including specific information will be considered an illegal act irrespective of if it is done electronically or in print. This extends to creating a secondary or tertiary copy of the work or a recorded copy and is only allowed with express written consent from the Publisher. All additional right reserved.

The information in the following pages is broadly considered to be a truthful and accurate account of facts and as such any inattention, use or misuse of the information in question by the reader will render any resulting actions solely under their purview. There are no scenarios in which the publisher or the original author of this work can be in any fashion deemed

Book One

Credit Score Repair

HOW TO REPAIR YOUR CREDIT AND BOOST YOUR SCORE FAST – DELETE JUDGMENTS, INQUIRIES AND NEGATIVE ACCOUNTS

THE COMPLETE CREDIT REPAIR EDITION

Fully Revised & Updated!

Table of Contents

Chapter 1..13
WHAT IS A FICO SCORE AND HOW IS IT
CALCULATED 13

Chapter 2 15
UNDERSTANDING YOUR CREDIT REPORT AND THE
CREDIT BUREAUS 15

Chapter 3 18
WHY YOU NEED A GOOD CREDIT SCORE TODAY 18

Chapter 4 21
HOW TO GET ALL YOUR REPORTS FOR FREE
ONLINE 21

Chapter 5 24
WHAT AFFECTS YOUR SCORE THE MOST 24

Chapter 6 27
YOU HAVE AN UNFAIR ADVANATAGE WITH THE
CONSUMER CREDIT LAWS – USE THEM 27

Chapter 7 30
HOW THE FAIR CREDIT ACTS PROTECT YOU 30

Chapter 8 33
BOOST YOUR SCORE IN 1 DAY BY OPTING OUT AT
THIS WEBSITE 33

Chapter 9 34
HOW TO REMOVE CREDIT INQUIRIES FAST.................34

Chapter 10 40
HOW TO REMOVE NEGATIVE ITEMS FAST....................40

Chapter 11 46
HOW TO DELETE PUBLIC COLLECTIONS AND
JUDGMENTS 46

Chapter 12..51
SECTION 609 CREDIT REPAIR METHOD 51

Chapter 13...54

FAST CREDIT REPAIR AFTER FORECLOSURE 54

Chapter 15 60

QUICK TECHNIQUES TO REBUILD CREDIT 60

Chapter 16 63

HOW TO GET LENDER OFFERS 63

Chapter 17 66

HOW TO BUILD BUSINESS CREDIT 66

Chapter 19 72

HOW TO NEGOTIATE AND SETTLE LARGE DEBTS 72

Chapter 20 75

MAINTAINING YOUR CREDIT 75

Chapter 21 78

FRAUD AND IDENTITY THEFT PREVENTION 78

Conclusion 85

"The Consumer Credit Laws Are In Favor Of the Debtor – Not the Creditor, But Most Americans Do Not Know This And Allow Strangers To Manipulate Their Credit Score and Report.

Forward by Author:

Why Did I Write This Book?

..In my late 20's I had some financial problems due to poor financial decisions, medical bills and SCHOOL LOANS that resulted in a pile of debt. This consequently then led to a terrible financial storm of public judgments and garnishments that destroyed my credit and depressed my lifestyle for several years because I did not know that I could negotiate with creditors and repair my credit.

My credit turnaround started when; at my lowest point, a friend I worked with gave me a simple book on how to repair my credit using consumer laws. I implemented some of the techniques with my own twists and creativity and achieved a 750 REAL score (the ones lenders see...not the fake ones you buy online) in only 1 year. It took me this long because I had OVER 12 bad accounts and over 5 public judgements, my credit was really bad.

..Today my FICO credit scores from all major bureaus hover between 810 and 830, for over 11 years.

As a former victim of bad credit, which was as low as 409 FICO at one point, I know all too well what it's like not having good credit:

- Having to deal in cash and money orders.
- Cashing my paychecks at check-checking stores.
- Not being able to rent a decent apartment.
- Rejected for cell phones and carriers.
- Insurance companies turning me down.
- Rejected by legitimate car finance companies.
- Potential employers not hiring me because I was a "financial risk"

When my credit turned really bad, I had a secure government job making $55,000+ a year, but couldn't even get insurance or rent a decent apartment. No one cared how much money or income I had; **it was ALL ABOUT THE CREDIT SCORE. To say this was frustrating is an understatement.**

Unfortunately, this is the American life.

<u>**Without good or fair credit you pay more**</u>, it's a "rigged" system set up to take advantage of people in certain financial circumstances.

BUT, you are not powerless; there is a flip side to this credit game. Many years ago our government gave us a way to get our credit back and protect it from sharks. But we have to do the work ourselves, and not trust someone else to do it for us.

Roughly 30 percent of all Americans are dealing with a poor credit score and more are falling into the trap of bad credit on a daily basis.

Introduction:

When you are at the bottom of a debt-shaped hole it can appear as though the deck is stacked against you and that you have no way of climbing your way out. This is quite simply not the case and the following chapters will discuss everything you need to know in order to get started on the path to an improved credit rating today.

You will learn about the basics including why you need good credit, what a FICO score is and how it is calculated, the things that affect your score the most and how to get your credit reports (all three of them) for free. You will also learn about the Fair Credit Reporting Act and other consumer protection laws and how they protect you. You will find out how to opt out of unwanted credit inquiries, remove those that are on your credit report and also remove a wide variety of negative items from your credit reports.

From there you will learn all about a variety of credit repair methods regardless of the situation that led to them. You will also how to get multiple offers from lenders, build credit with a small business and how to stop collectors in their tracks and negotiate and settle debts of varying sizes. Finally, you will learn how to maintain good credit and prevent identity theft or fraud from ruining your hard work.

There are plenty of books on this subject on the market, thanks again for choosing this one Every effort was made to ensure it is full of as much useful information as possible and we offer free letter templates and articles on our website.

Chapter 1

WHAT IS A FICO SCORE AND HOW IS IT CALCULATED

Your FICO score is a measure of the overall quality of your credit that was developed by the Fair Isaac Corporation which is a software company that focuses on analytics and works with businesses in more than 90 countries around the world. While it is not the only available metric for determining credit score, it is the one that is most commonly used by a wide range of different lenders and companies when it comes to determining the level of risk that is associated with a given individual.

The calculations that go into determining a person's credit score are proprietary which means that the Fair Isaac Company doesn't share them with anyone. However, some of the details regarding it have been found out, including the fact that a FICO score is based on a handful of difference categories of various levels of importance to the total. It has been determined that payment history is weighted with approximately 35 percent relevance, amount owed has a 30 percent relevance, credit history length has a 15 percent relevance, abundance of new credit has a 10 percent relevance and type of credit used has a 10 percent relevance.

Payment history relates to how prompt you have been when it comes to previous payments you have made to various creditors. It also factors in things such as delinquency, number of accounts you have in collections, bankruptcy and how long it has been since these problems appeared on your record. As such, the greater number of problems that you have had in this regard, the worse your overall FICO score is going to be.

When it comes to the amount you current owe to lenders, FICO takes into account the amount of debt you currently have as well as the types of accounts you hold and the number of different accounts that you currently hold. This section also looks at your current financial situation as a whole which means the more debt you currently have the weaker your score will be.

The other areas that FICO looks into are all relatively self-explanatory. Overall, the longer you go without having anything negative added to your credit history, the better your overall FICO score is going to be. It is also important to keep in mind that your FICO score will only take into account information that has been added to your credit report which is not the sum total of information that a lender will look at while determining if you are eligible for a loan or what your rates will be

Chapter 2

UNDERSTANDING YOUR CREDIT REPORT AND THE CREDIT BUREAUS

Your credit report is actually more complicated than it may appear at first glance, simply because you are actually dealing with reports from three different agencies, TransUnion, Experian and Equifax. What this means is that you will need to check each of the three reports on a regular basis to ensure you have all the pertinent information on your current credit score.

Anatomy of a credit report

While the three major credit reports are going to vary somewhat, information is always going to be grouped into four major categories, these are credit inquires, creditor information, public record information and personal information.

Personal information: The personal information section is going to include things like you name and any aliases you use, your social security number, date of birth, employment information and your current and previous addresses.

Public record information: This section will include any currently pending legal issues related to your current financial situation. This can include bankruptcies, wage garnishments, judgements and liens. A TransUnion report will also show the approximate date when these details will be removed from your report.

Creditor information: This section will show all of your debts that have been turned over to a collection agency and all of the lines of credit that you currently have. Additionally, you will find details outlining the status of the account in question, if you share responsibility on any of the accounts, your current balance, payment history, credit limit and if the account is currently past due. Typically, positive and negative accounts will be grouped together.

If you have accounts that are negatively affecting your credit, it is important to keep in mind that you can dispute any of these issues with the credit reporting company. Barring that they will fall off your report after the issue has been resolved for seven years.

Each of your accounts can be classified in the following ways: if any of your accounts are listed as charged off, that means that the account has been written off from the creditor as a loss. While this means you may not have to pay off the account, it will still show up on your credit report for seven years. A revolving account is the classification given to credit cards, you don't need to pay these in full each month and can instead revolve them and just pay the interest.

An installment account is the classification given to loans or other accounts that involved fixed payments. An open account is the classification given to accounts that force you to pay the total balance off each month. A collection account is the classification given to any account that has been transferred to a debt collection agency, this will even show on accounts that you have settled the debt for in the past seven years.

Credit inquiries: This section of your credit report includes a list of every agency that has reviewed your credit report in the past seven years. There are two different types of inquiries, hard inquiries are made by lenders when you apply for a line of credit, too many of these in a seven-year period can negatively impact your credit score. Soft inquiries are made by you or agencies that preapprove you for lines of credit.

Credit report codes: The following is a list of codes you may see on your credit report and what they mean.

- CURR ACCT: This means the account is in good standing and current.
- CUR WAS 30-2: This means the account is currently in good standing but has been late by 30 days or more at least twice.
- PAID: This means the account is currently inactive and has been paid off
- CHARGOFF: This means the account has been charged off.
- COLLECT: This means the account has been sent to collections.
- BKLIQREQ: This means the debt has been forgiven due to bankruptcy.
- DELINQ 60: This means the account is at least 60 days past due.

Chapter 3

WHY YOU NEED A GOOD CREDIT SCORE TODAY

These days, society is increasingly dependent on credit scores when it comes to making a wide variety of different decisions about your future. As such, if your credit isn't as good as you might like, it will affect more than just your rates on a loan or if you are eligible for a credit card. Your credit is essentially a history that shows how strict you have been when it comes to reliably paying bills on time in the past which means a wide variety of different individuals are going to be curious about it as a way of determining how you are likely to act in the future.

Your credit score can vacillate from 350, indicating you are an extremely high-risk investment, to 850, which indicates anyone who loans you money is almost certain to get it back. Additionally, your credit rating is typically shown via a numerical rating from 1 (very bad) to 9 (very good). Currently only about five percent of Americans have a credit rating of 500 or lower while about fifteen percent have a score above 800 with the majority falling between the 700 and 800 range.

Living arrangements: First and foremost, your credit score affects your ability to get a mortgage and what you will pay monthly and overall. A poor credit rating can also prevent you from successfully getting a mortgage at all, or even prevent landlords from renting to you as well. This is due to the fact that many landlords consider a lease a type of loan, after all, they are loaning you're a place to live in exchange for rent each month. If you have a low credit rating, and they do decide to rent to you, be prepared to pay extra for the privilege of having a roof over your head.

Car payments: The quality of your credit will also affect whether you will be approved for a loan for the car you are interested in purchasing as well as what your interest rate is going to be. In this case, bad credit can limit your options as fewer lenders will be willing to work with you and those that do are generally going to charge more to balance out the risk you represent. This typically translates into repayments for longer periods of time (72 months as opposed to 60 or less) and higher overall payments each month.

Job search: While the first two scenarios are to be expected, many people will be surprised to learn that a low credit score can affect your employment prospects as well. While employers can't check credit scores, they can check credit reports and many do so as a routine part of the hiring process. Depending on the job, if you have a history of poor financial responsibility an employer may be hesitant to offer you the position you have been dreaming about. Likewise, when it comes to promotions, many companies check credit reports to ensure their executives won't give the company a bad name.

Starting a business: Those who are grinding away at a 9-to-5 aren't the only ones who need to worry about their credit score, if you are self-employed a negative credit score can have even more serious implications. If you are looking to start a business with a small business loan, then you can bet lenders will check your credit score and, as most new businesses tend to fail, they will be very selective about who they lend their money to.

Monthly bills: Your credit score will also have an effect on many of your monthly bills including your utilities. Utility companies loan you their services every month and if your credit report shows that you are a risky investment then they will most definitely charge you more for the privilege of having electricity, running water, cellular service or cable and internet.

Chapter 4

HOW TO GET ALL YOUR REPORTS FOR FREE ONLINE

Every single American citizen is entitled to one free copy of each of their credit reports every twelve months. The Fair Credit Reporting Act (FCRA) means that TransUnion, Experian and Equifax are obligated to provide you with these details, but only if you ask for them. The FCRA promotes the privacy and accuracy of the information from these credit reporting agencies and is enforced by the Federal Trade Commission.

To order your free reports, all you have to do is visit AnnualCreditReport.com, fill out an Annual Credit Request Form (available at Consumer.FTC.gov) and mail it to Annual Credit Report Request Service, P.O. Box 105281, Atlanta, GA 30348-5281 or call 1-877-322-8228.

Assuming you visit the website, you will be sent to a form page where you will be required to include pertinent identifying information including your date of birth, social security number, address and name. If you have moved within the previous two years you will likely need to provide your previous address as well. Once you submit these details you will then be taken to a page that will allow you to select the reports you wish to receive, you can choose to get all three at once or to get them one at a time, it doesn't matter as long as you haven't received them in the previous 12 months.

You will then be taken to a page that will further help to verify your identity. You will receive a list of questions about the terms of your loans, your current creditors, and the like, that only you are likely to know. You will need to answer all the questions correctly which means you may need to have your current bill and loan statements handy.

There are pros and cons to pulling all three reports at once or waiting and spacing them out. If you decide to get your reports one at a time then you can space them out throughout the year, one every four months, so that you will always be aware when something new affects your credit, negatively or positively. The downside is that if there is something negative on one of your credit reports and not the others, then you will have to wait a full year to find out about it.

On the other hand, pulling all three of your credit reports at the same time will allow you to pinpoint any issues right away which means you can start working toward a solution for them as soon as possible. Additionally, this method will allow you to determine what the differences between the various reports are and if there are any discrepancies that can be easily resolved such as one of them not showing that you have finished paying off a loan. The downside is, of course, that if something happens to your credit in the next eleven months you won't know about it until the time comes to pull all three again. To mitigate this fact, you can sign up with a credit monitoring service, which will keep tabs on your credit for you in between the periods where you are eligible for a free copy of your various reports.

Be aware of imposters
While AnnualCreditReport.com is the only legitimate way to pull your credit reports on a regular basis for free, that doesn't mean it is the only site out there offering this service. While these other sites might have offers for free services, they likely

come with strings attached, at best, or are simply scams designed to steal your personal information, at worst. Especially be aware of sites whose URLs are misspellings of AnnualCreditReport.com as it is unlikely that they have anything remotely close to benign intentions in mind.

Additionally, you are going to want to keep in mind that AnnualCreditReport.com verifies all of your information directly on the site which means that if you receive an email claiming to be from this site then it is likely a form of phishing that is trying to steal your personal information. Likewise, the three major credit reporting agencies never contact individuals directly which means if you receive a phone call or email from someone claiming to be with either TransUnion, Experian or Equifax then the safest choice is just to ignore it.

Chapter 5

WHAT AFFECTS YOUR SCORE THE MOST

There are six factors that have the most bearing on your credit score which means it will behoove you to keep an eye on all of them if you hope to retain a score as close to 850 as possible.

Credit card utilization: Your credit card utilization rate is how much credit you have available compared to how much you are currently using at any one time. It can be determined by simply dividing your credit card balances by the total limits of all of your credit cards. As such, it is beneficial to apply for a number of credit cards, even if you don't ever intend on using them. It is important to keep in mind that this amount is not calculated based on the balance that is on any one card which means you don't need to worry about maintaining a balance and rolling it over from month to month. It is always a better idea to pay off any credit card purchases as the end of the month instead.

On-time payments: Paying your bills on time is one of the easiest ways to ensure you maintain a healthy credit rating. It is weighted very heavily when it comes to influencing your credit card score which means that if you miss a few payments your score is very likely to suffer as a result.

Derogatory marks: Derogatory marks on your credit score include liens, foreclosures, bankruptcies and accounts that are in collections. Each of these will affect your credit rating significantly, with bankruptcies and foreclosures being the most serious. Derogatory marks will stay on your record for up to ten years and, assuming they are accurate, there is little you can do about removing them early. The average amount a derogatory mark will decrease your credit is 50 points.

The monetary amount that lead to the derogatory mark doesn't matter when it comes to your credit rating which means that have a single dollar sent to collections will still ding your credit 50 points. The date of the derogatory mark does matter, however, and it is based on when the negative action took place, not when it occurred. For example, if you defaulted on a debt in 2012 but the account wasn't sent to collections until 2017 then it will be listed as a recent derogatory mark and the seven-year timeframe will start in 2017, not 2012. Additionally, it is important to keep in mind that the derogatory mark will stay on your record regardless of whether or not you have since paid off the outstanding lien or collection amount.

Credit line age: The average age of your lines of credit simply refers to how long you have been building credit for. Lenders like to see that you have a long history of successfully managing credit as it makes it easier to determine if you are a risky investment or not. The longer your credit history, the more likely it is that you have been able to successfully manage your credit. As such, it is never a good idea to close out old credit card accounts, even if you don't use them anymore. Not only will this decrease your total amount of available credit, it will shrink your credit line age average as well. This doesn't just apply to credit cards but also to personal loans, student loans, auto loans and mortgages as well.

Number of accounts: As a general rule, the more lines of credit you have, the higher your credit score will be as it shows you have been given credit by more lenders. Ideally you will want to have a mix of installment and revolving credit lines for the best results. This doesn't mean you will want to go out and open as many credit cards as possible, however, as this factor weighs less heavily on your score than most.

Number of hard credit inquiries: Each time a lender checks your credit score for things like a mortgage, credit card, personal or business loan, student loan or auto loan, it will negatively affect your credit score by a few points. This effect typically wears off after a few months as long as you don't make a habit of promoting these types of checks. The effect is cumulative, however, and having multiple hard credit inquiries in a short period of time is not recommended.

Chapter 6

YOU HAVE AN UNFAIR ADVANATAGE WITH THE CONSUMER CREDIT LAWS – USE THEM

The Fair Credit Acts

When you are going about trying to fix your credit, it can often feel as though the deck is stacked against you, however, the truth of the matter is that there are several laws that can help you to even the odds when it comes to dealing with both creditors and credit bureaus.

FCRA: The FCRA does more than just provide you with a free credit report each year, it also regulates the various credit reporting organizations and helps to ensure that the information they gather on you is both accurate and fair. This means that if you see inaccurate information on your credit report, and report it to the relevant agency, they are legally required to look into the matter and resolve it, typically within 30 days. The same applies to agencies or organizations that generally add details to your credit report. Finally, if an organization that reviews your credit report decides to charge your more or declines to do business with you based on what they find in your report, they are legally obligated to let you know why and what report they found the negative information in.

While this won't help you with that particular lender, if the information is inaccurate you will at least know where to go to clear up the issue. Additionally, if you report an inaccuracy and the credit reporting agency ignores your request you can sue them to recover the damages or a minimum of $2,500. You may also be able to win an additional amount based on punitive damages and legal fees and any other associated costs. You must file legal proceedings within 5 years of when this occurs.

Fair Credit Billing Act: This federal law is part of what is known as the Truth in Lending Act. Its purpose is to provide safeguards to consumers when it comes to unfair billing and make it clear how any errors must be corrected. This law is useful if you are charged for things you didn't purchase, are charged an inaccurate amount for products or services, you didn't receive and item you paid for, payments made aren't reflected in amounts owed or if your statements are sent to an inaccurate address.

To take advantage of this law, the first thing you need to do is to send a physical letter to the billing inquiries address that the creditor provides. You need to ensure the creditor receives your letter within 60 days from the date the error shows up on your statement. Some creditors allow for disputes to be handled online but utilizing this option can nullify your rights through this law so it is not recommended. The creditor will then have 30 days to acknowledge they received your letter and 90 days to either correct the mistake or tell you why they think it is valid. If they turn down your request you are then allowed to ask for all the documentation saying why they turned you down.

A subset of this law is what is known as the Hidden Gem Law, this means you can dispute any transaction made within 100 miles of your home, or anywhere in your home state, which exceeds $50. As long as you make a good faith effort to dispute the transaction, and return the item or stop using the service, then the company will likely refund the transaction.

Fair Debt Collection Practices Act: This is another law that benefits consumers when it comes to debt collector actions. This includes not only debt collection agencies but also their attorneys. This law prevents debt collection agencies from contacting you if you have requested that the debt be validated, contacting you instead of your attorney (if applicable) calling before 8 am or after 9 pm, contacting you at work, calling constantly, reporting false information to credit bureaus, embarrassing you in an effort to collect the debt, adding your name to a list of debtors, threatening legal action they can't actually follow through on, misrepresentation or contacting you after you have sent a letter requesting that they stop or saying that you will not pay the debt in question.

If the debt collector breaks these rules or acts in other ways they are not allowed then you can file a private lawsuit and be recouped costs, fees and damages. What's more, you don't even need to prove damages and you will likely be awarded a minimum of $1,000.

Chapter 7

HOW THE FAIR CREDIT ACTS PROTECT YOU

The FCRA is a complicated law that bears looking into a little more deeply. Likewise, just because it protects you in a wide variety of ways doesn't mean the credit reporting agency or creditors are always going to follow it the way they should. What follows are several common ways the FCRA is violated on a regular basis. If you feel as though your rights have been violated in any of these ways refer to the previous chapter.

Reporting or furnishing old information: While credit bureaus and creditors are required to keep your details as up to date as possible, you will frequently find that they fail to do so in several key ways. They will frequently fail to report that a given debt was discharged because bankruptcy was filed, that an old debt is either re-engaged or completely new, report that a closed account is active when it has actually been closed or keep information that is older than seven years (ten for bankruptcies) on your credit report. If you report these errors they are legally required to look into them within 30 days.

Reporting blatantly inaccurate information: Creditors are not allowed to provide information to credit bureaus that they know, or should know, is inaccurate. This includes classifying a debt as charged off when it was really paid in full, altering balances due, reporting a timely payment as late, listing you as the debtor when you were only an authorized user on a specific account and failing to mention when identity fraud was suspected or confirmed for a given account. Again, if you report these errors they are legally required to look into them.

Mixing up files: While it may seem surprising, credit reporting agencies frequently mix up files on individuals, potentially harming your credit score for someone else's mistakes. These issues can arise between individuals who have similar social security numbers, if you are a Junior or a Senior and the issue is with the other person's credit, mixing up details when names are similar or even mixing up details for two people with the same zip code.

Violations of debt dispute with credit reporting agencies: As previously discussed, credit reporting agencies have to follow strict rules when it comes to handling disputes; nevertheless, there are frequently issues with the ways they follow through on the process. This includes failing to notify you that a dispute has been received, failing to conduct an investigation into the dispute in a timely fashion and failing to correct disputes in a timely fashion.

Creditor debt dispute violations: The FCRA also has strict rules when it comes to how creditors must handle disputes, which are frequently disregarded. These violations include things like not notifying credit reporting agencies that a debt is being disputed, not submitting corrected information after the debt has been successfully disputed, not conducting internal investigations into the dispute once they have been notified of the error, making it difficult to submit disputes and not informing you of the results of the investigation into the dispute within five days after it has been completed.

Inaccurate credit report requests: Just because certain individuals are allowed to see your credit report doesn't mean they are allowed to do so at all times. The FCRA ensures that your credit report can't be accessed in order to determine if you are worth filing a lawsuit against, can't be accessed by employers without express permission, and can't be accessed by previous creditors related to debts that have been discharged for bankruptcy just to see what your current financial activity is.

Chapter 8

BOOST YOUR SCORE IN 1 DAY BY OPTING OUT AT THIS WEBSITE

OptOutPrescreen.com is a website that can allow you to opt out of offers from insurers and creditors that come in the mail offering to "preapprove" you for this or that. Taking advantage of this site to opt out of these offers will, in turn, prevent credit reporting agencies from providing your information to these companies. On this site, you can choose to opt out for five years, opt out permanently or opt back in if you change your mind. Be aware that this will only stop you from being subject to soft-credit inquiries which do not affect your credit score nearly as much (if at all) as hard credit inquiries.

You can opt out electronically for five years or permanently opt out by sending in your details in the mail. If you decide to opt out electronically you will need to provide your name, social security number, date of birth, current address and telephone number. If you decide to opt out permanently you will need to enter the same information online before being provided with a form to print off and mail.

Opting out can usually increase your score 2-7 points overnight.

Chapter 9

HOW TO REMOVE CREDIT INQUIRIES FAST

The Basics

Hard credit inquiries will automatically be removed from your credit report after two years. If you don't want to wait that long, you can take the following steps to remove them in a more timely fashion.

Step 1: The first thing you are going to want to do is to order your credit reports and check the inquiry section, which is generally near the bottom of the report. It is important to remember that soft inquiries, such as those that will lead you to be preapproved for offers or services will not affect your credit rating in most cases. As such you are going to want to focus on those inquiries by organizations that will actually grant you credit instead. You will ideally recognize the names of these organizations, but now and then you might come across those that are a mystery to you as well.

Step 2: Once you know what you are looking for, the next thing you are going to want to do is to find the address of each of the creditors. This information will be listed on an Experian credit report but not on Equifax or TransUnion. If the creditor doesn't show up on the Experian credit report but they do show up on the others the easiest way to get the address of the creditor is to call the credit bureau and ask for it. It is unlikely you will be able to get in touch with a live person from TransUnion, though Equifax lists an 800 number on all of their reports.

Step 3: Once you have the address in hand, the next thing you will need to do is prepare a letter asking each creditor to remove their inquiry. The FCRA ensures that only authorized inquiries will show up on your credit report which means in order to get them removed you need to challenge whether the creditor in question has authorization to pull your details. You should also send a letter to the credit bureau in question and ask that they remove the inquiry. The sample letter is below:

Date

Name
Address

(Credit Bureau Name/Creditor Name)
Address

Re: Unauthorized Credit Request

Dear (Credit Bureau Name/Creditor Name),

I recently received my (credit bureau name) credit report and I saw there was a credit inquiry from (Creditor Name) that I believe is unauthorized. I did not authorize this credit inquiry prior to it taking place which means it should not show up on my credit history. I am writing this letter to ask that you remove it from my file, as well as instigate an investigation into (Creditor Name) to determine the details behind this inquiry. When this inquiry has been completed I ask that you take the necessary steps to remove it from my file ASAP. Furthermore, I ask that you send me the documentation that will let me know that this inquiry has been removed. If you find that this inquiry was authorized, I ask that you send me proof of the authorization as well.

Thank you for your time

(Signature)

(Include credit report in question)

Step 4: Sometimes the credit bureau or creditor will just remove the inquiry without doing a full inquiry, which should be your goal. Other times they will do their due diligence and return to you the documentation that you signed giving the creditor access to your credit report. When you receive this documentation, it is important that you read it over carefully and look for any ambiguity in the wording, possibly even taking it to a lawyer depending on how badly you want the inquiry removed.

If you find some wiggle room, be sure to write back to the bureau and argue your case. Alternately, you may argue that the form was too difficult for the layman to understand. You can also threaten to contact the Banking Commission and file a complaint about the authorization form if it is not removed from your report.

Creditors will frequently ignore these requests which is why it is important to send every letter via Certified Mail and keep any receipts you receive. **If the creditor does not respond in 30 days you can then call and demand action or take legal action as described in chapter 6. If they don't respond, whether or not you authorized the inquiry becomes functionally irrelevant because they have not responded to the dispute.** Always hold you ground and demand that the inquiry be removed ASAP and make it clear that you will take the issue to the authorities if they do not comply. Keep in mind that every inquiry you have removed early will increase your credit score by several points.

"Secret" Inquiry Removal Strategies

Mail Certified Letters to the Creditor

This is the most effective strategy as the Creditor is the one actually reporting the negative information or responsible for the credit inquiry on your report.

Mail Certified Letters to the Repositories (Credit Bureaus)

This is not as effective anymore because the bureau will just send you a letter back that it is up to the Creditor to delete or remove inquiries. By law you can request the credit Bureau do an investigation but all they generally do is call the Creditor and verify if the inquiry was made.

Make sure you reference the Fair Credit Reporting Acts in the letters and state that the inquiry in question is invalid, unauthorized and you want it deleted immediately.

Both creditor and credit bureau only have 30 days to respond to your dispute, if they do not respond within the 30 day limit, they have to remove the inquiry by law; however, some states have recently changed this law and removed the 30 day requirement for Bureau and Creditor, unfortunately. Please be sure to check your States laws regarding the 30 day limit (a Google search will work)

When I was removing my credit inquiries, 2 out of 12 did not respond in the 30 day limit, and they were Credit bureaus not creditor, so I sent them the certified mail return receipts and proof and they had no choice but to remove the inquiries.

Why Send Certified Mail?

Because you will stand out and get attention, hardly anyone send postal mail anymore. When removing over a dozen inquiries in a month, I used certified USPS mail and I send letters to the Credit Bureaus, creditor and creditor company OWNER, which can be found by doing some research into online corporate records.

Here is a little secret most people don't know – Creditors almost always break the Fair Credit Acts because they are so vast and complex, it is nearly impossible to adhere to all of the Acts, and most court actions end in favor of the Debtor, if the Debtor challenges them, shows up and uses the Consumer laws to their rightful advantage.

If you are persistent and push your claim, you have a high chance of succeeding. But, most people DO NOT do this or they hire a credit agency to do it for them for a large ridiculous fee, and the agency doesn't do it correctly, how can they when they have 100 other people who need credit repair as well.

Chapter 10

HOW TO REMOVE NEGATIVE ITEMS FAST

While most issues will be removed from your credit report in seven years, (ten for bankruptcies) you may not have to wait that long if you do your due diligence. It doesn't matter if it is a foreclosure, charge off, bill in collections or late payments, they all have the potential to be removed early.

Check for errors: Studies show that more than fifty percent of all credit reports contain errors of some kind. These errors might not be major, such as including details from someone else's report, they may be smaller, and thus easier to miss. This means you are going to want to check the specifics of every entry and ensure it matches up with your personal records. You are going to want to check every credit limit, balance, payment status, account status, open and close date and account number and note any errors.

Once the errors are noted, you will then want to send a letter to each credit bureau outlining the mistakes and requesting that they are removed. You can use the letter outlined in the previous chapter and substitute in the errors you have found for the part about credit inquiries. The good part about this is that if the bureau can't determine the accuracy of the information it will simply be removed.

Goodwill letter: If you can't find any inaccuracies, or the bureau verified the ones you pointed out as correct, you can instead try sending what is known as a goodwill letter. You will send this letter to the collection agency or to the creditor and ask that they remove the negative entry based on goodwill. This will be most effective if you are looking to have charge offs, collections or late payments removed. In this letter, you will want to explain your situation to the agency in question and ask that they essentially help you out by removing the offending information. While this may seem like a long shot, it works a surprising amount of the time, especially with regards to late payments. This method is especially effective if you are a current customer and the organization has a reason to want to hold on to your business. A sample goodwill letter is below:

Date

(Creditor/Collection Agency Name)
(Creditor/Collection Agency Address)

Re: Account number provided

To whom it may concern:

I am writing regarding an issue I recently came across in my credit report (list specifics) that I was hoping you could help me to rectify. I understand that making payments on time is very important and that failing to do so causes issues for your company. If you look at my file you will see that I have done so a majority of the time I have been a client of your company and that my (late/missing) payment is an exception, not a rule. I missed the payment in question do to an (unavoidable emergency real or imagined, the more detail the better) and while I tried to make the payment on time I was unable to do so.

I can guarantee that the issue won't happen again as my (financial, physical, emotional) state has improved dramatically since (issue) and it is no longer a factor when it comes to making payments. As a courtesy, I am requesting that you make this goodwill adjustment to my record in light of my history of on time payments. This will allow me to improve my credit score and boost my confidence in being a (company name) customer.

I appreciate your time
(Signature)

Pay for delete: If you are dealing with charge offs or unpaid collections, the most effective way to have them removed from your account is to negotiate with the creditor directly and offer to pay a portion of what you owe in exchange for having the negative entry DELETED from your report. If you go down this path it is important that you get the agreement in writing prior to making the payment as once the payment is made you lose all of your leverage. A sample letter outlining this process can be found below.

Date
Collection Agency/Creditor Name
Account number:
Amount owed:

To whom it may concern,

I am writing to you in reference to the above account number in an effort to settle the amount due in a way that will benefit us both. This letter should not be seen as an acknowledgement of liability to the debt in question and I shall still retain the right to request verification of the debt from your company if the terms outlined below aren't acceptable to you. With that being said, however, I am willing to pay off (percentage of amount) of the debt as a sign of good faith based on the following conditions:

- Your company will put forth the effort to successfully remove all references to this issue from the (credit bureaus that list the issue).
- Moving forward your company will not list the debt as a settled account.
- The payment made will be considered payment in full of the debt in question.
- The debt will not be transferred or sold to a different creditor.
- This agreement will not be made public in any way, shape or form.

In exchange for these written assurances I will pay (amount about fifty percent for new accounts and thirty percent for older accounts) as soon as I receive an appropriate response. This should not be taken as a promise to pay, rather it is a restricted settlement offer based solely on your agreement to the terms outlined above. Prior to making any payments I will need a written acceptance of these terms on your company letterhead that is signed by an authorized representative of your company.

This offer will expire in 30 days, I look forward to a prompt response.

Regards,
(Typed Name)

..More Secret Removal Strategies

Not recommended for the reader – seek legal advice

I once had 3 credit cards that were charged off and unpaid. I sent strong letters to the credit card company and they agreed to settle but not delete the accounts.

I wanted them deleted.

I decided to look into filing a federal lawsuit pro se. I reasoned that if I can show them how serious I was and that my basis was provable in court (Credit Billing Act violations), then they would yield to my demand.

I did some research and discovered that I could file a claim in the nearest US court under Federal Question, since the Fair Credit acts are under the federal; jurisdiction. I typed up my own docket using previous cases as a template, mailed it to the Credit Card Company and credit bureaus and demanded damages of $1,000,000.

At the time I had NO CLUE what I was doing but it worked; I was so inexperienced that instead of actually filing the claim, I simply sent it to the credit card company's legal department and the credit bureau's dispute department, but with one extra step.

I also searched out the OWNER and the Statutory Agent of the credit card company by searching through the corporate records of the state they were headquartered in, and included their names in my self-created docket. **Anyone can find this**

information by searching for the respective states' Secretary of State Office, corporate division.

In about 10 days I received a call from the Credit Card Company's legal firm representative. He was very calm on the phone and basically said that he tried looking my docket-case up in the Clerk online for the Ohio Northern US Court District and found nothing.

He then proceeded to state to me that he could file a suit back against my for malicious attempt, but then ended the sentence that his client wants this done and over with now, so they are prepared to delete ALL charged off credit card accounts if I agree to not sue them or follow through with the claim!

Obviously I signed their letter stating this and in about 30 days the bureaus refreshed their data and the accounts were gone and my score INCREASED 202 Points!

My original goal was never to go to court but merely to settle before that.

I do not recommend you do extreme tactics like this unless you feel it really is justified, and even then be sure to seek legal advice. There are a lot of details that would go into this, let alone acting pro se.

Credit repair is very personal and unique to each person, each case is different. I was willing to do extreme measures to get what I wanted so that I could get a mortgage loan at the time and buy a house.

Chapter 11

HOW TO DELETE PUBLIC COLLECTIONS AND JUDGMENTS

Public records that appear on your credit report include civil judgments, tax liens and bankruptcy filings.

Tax liens: the first thing you are going to want to do is to ensure that the debt has been paid in full. Next, you are going to want to go ahead and prepare to file a dispute. The federal government has a Fresh Start program that makes this process fairly straightforward. To qualify you are going to need to be current on your taxes and have received a Release of Tax Lien document. You will also need the original form that provided notice of the lien in the first place. You will then need to fill out IRS form 12277 Application for Withdrawal of Filed form 688Y, available at IRS.gov. You will then need to submit this, along with your original form and proof that you have paid off the lien to the IRS. You should then receive IRS form 10916(c) which states that the federal lien has been withdrawn. Finally, you will submit a copy of that form to the credit bureaus with a request that they remove the inaccurate information from your report.

Judgements: Having a judgement on your credit report can be nearly as harmful as having a repossession or a loan default. While removing a judgement is possible, it is not as easy as removing a late payment or a credit inquiry. A judgement shows up on your credit report if a judge signs off on a statement saying that you owe a specific debt. This occurs when a lawsuit is filed against you for the purpose of collecting a debt, even if you weren't aware of the court proceedings at the time. It is important to keep in mind that just because a judgement was issued against you, that doesn't mean the other party was paid, which is a fact that you will use to your advantage.

There are two different ways to deal with a judgement once it has hit your credit report, you can have the judgement dismissed, also known as vacated, or remove the judgment from your credit report. If you take this second route you can contact the other party with the letter used to settle an outstanding debt from the previous chapter.

Dismiss a judgement: In order to have a judgement dismissed, you need to file a motion to dismiss the judgment with the court that issued the judgement in the first place. This is essentially an appeal that states the original outcome was inaccurate or unfair based on a specific number of reasons. First you will want to look through the proceedings and ensure that the person who requested the judgement in the first place went ahead and followed all the correct procedures and laws for doing so in your area. If there was mismanagement of this process, the odds are that the judge didn't know about it when the judgement was made.

In addition to following up on the judgement process, you will need to ensure that the person filing the judgement also followed proper court proceedings as you may be able to win out based on a technicality. This is especially important if you failed to show up for your court date and the plaintiff won by default as long as you had a valid reason for not showing up for the hearing in the first place. Again, it is important to familiarize yourself with local laws for this process to be effective.

When you prepare your motion to vacate it is important you follow local rules for civil procedure to the letter, the rules for your area should spell out exactly what you need to do, explain valid reasons a judgment can be vacated and will often include specific language you will need to use to file your motion.

The document you create should explain why the judgement should be vacated, starting with the reasons why you are bringing the motion forward. You will need to state your procedural defense and explain why you missed the original hearing if that is what happened. Valid reasons include that you were not served properly, that you responded to the summons but there was no initial judgment or that you did not have time to make it to the hearing based on when you were served. There may be other valid reasons in your area as well.

You will also need to include reasons why the judgement would have been dismissed if you had been at the hearing including things like, the collection agency failed to respond to your validation request or that the debt amount exceed local usury interest limits.

Bankruptcy: Removing a bankruptcy from your credit report is the most difficult black mark to remove. While it is far from a sure thing, a general rule is that the older the bankruptcy is, the easier it is to remove. To get started you are going to want to look for errors relating to it, if there are then you are in luck. If you find errors you can go about asking the bureau to remove them in the standard way.

Regardless if the information is accurate or not, you are still going to want to ask the bureau to verify the bankruptcy as they will be unlikely to go about doing it in the right way. Assuming they come back and tell you that it has been verified by one court or another, this is almost always inaccurate as courts rarely verify bankruptcies. With this information in hand, you will want to reach out to the court that has been specified and ask them how they verify bankruptcies. You can call and ask for this information, typically from the clerk of the court. Assuming they explain that they don't verify bankruptcies you will then want to get that fact in writing.

When you receive this letter in the mail, you will then want to send it to the bureau that claimed to have verified your bankruptcy in the first place along with a letter explaining what it is and stating that, as the bankruptcy was not actually verified, you want it taken off your record as by not doing so previously, but saying that they did, they are in direct violation of the FCRA.

Deletion of Negative Public Records (Judgments)

Ever had your wages garnished?

I did – I fought – I won

I had to pay a settlement, but I got the judgement VACATED from the clerk of court and removed completely from my credit record.

Garnishments are the worst thing for your credit, you don't want this on your report, and any potential employers will have a serious problem with this.

I used whatever leverage I could find and wrote a letter to the Judge that handled the case and explained in lengthy detail how it all happened, why the creditor was being too harsh and ruthless and what violations I believed the committed.

The Judge actually ruled in my favor for the second hearing which I could not attend due to work, I gave my letter to the bailiff before the court date.

I still had to pay court costs but I won. I wasn't even there, and the Creditor's attorney was very upset, apparently he losing the case really made him look bad to the firms' Partners.

Public Records will require serious measures to get vacated or deleted. **Keep in mind anything is negotiable if you can find the leverage or violation within the Fair Credit Acts. Most of the time they are there, but you have to look very hard.**

In addition, getting creditors to vacate or delete a public judgement can be accomplished with settlements and negotiations while leveraging the Fair Credit Acts. Where there is a will there is a way. Do you think attorneys give up when the odds are stacked against their case? No way, they find loopholes and any leverage they can find – I would suggest you view defending your credit report the same way, only the consumer laws are MORE biased for you.

Chapter 12

SECTION 609 CREDIT REPAIR METHOD

To understand how the Section 609 credit repair method works, it is important to understand that the FCRA was written before the advent of the internet. As such, they require the credit reporting agencies to have physical copies of all documentation to support each account that is being reported on. This is a problem for these agencies as virtually all credit items added to your credit report these days are submitted electronically. This, in turn, means that it is rare for any documents to be reviewed prior to changes being made to your credit report.

Essentially, the credit reporting agencies just give all creditors the benefit of the doubt when new information is added to your file. You can use this to your advantage by asking for hard-copy verification via Section 609 of the FCRA for virtually anything negative that is listed on your credit report. You simply need to use the following letter and not be deterred by any scare tactics that the credit reporting agencies will use to cover their tracks as they will try everything in their power to avoid having to tell you that they don't have the physical documentation.

With the following letter, you will need to be sure to always include a copy of a photo identification as well as a copy of your social security card(also include your past residences for 5 years). **This is due to the fact that the FCRA only requires the credit reporting agencies to respond to individuals in writing if they provide these details.** Without it, your letters will simply be ignored. When disputing accounts, it is also important to never dispute more than 22 at one time. This is the magic number, anything more than that will cause you dispute to be considered frivolous. **Additionally, you will want to ensure you hand label your envelopes as type envelopes will be opened far less often.**

Name

Address

(Credit Bureau Name)

Date

To Whom It May Concern:

This letter is a formal complaint that you are reporting inaccurate and incomplete credit information. I am distressed that you have included the below information in my credit profile and have failed to maintain reasonable procedures in your operations to assure maximum possible accuracy in the credit reports you publish.

Credit reporting laws ensure that bureaus report only 100% accurate credit information. Every step must be taken to assure the information reported is completely accurate and correct. The following information therefore needs to be re-investigated. I respectfully request to be provided proof that these inquiries were in fact authorized with an instrument bearing my signature, and for legitimate business purposes. Failing that, the unauthorized inquiry must be deleted from the report as soon as possible:

(Accounts you wish to have removed from your report)

Please delete this misleading information, and supply a corrected credit profile to all creditors who have received a copy within the last 6 months, or the last 2 years for employment purposes.

Additionally, please provide the name, address, and telephone number of each credit grantor or other subscriber.

Under federal law, you have 30 days to complete your re-investigation. Be advised that the description of the procedure used to determine the accuracy and completeness of the information is hereby requested as well, to be provided within 15 days of the completion of your re-investigation.

Sincerely,

(Signature)

Name

SSN#

Chapter 13

FAST CREDIT REPAIR AFTER FORECLOSURE

While rebuilding your credit after a foreclosure is difficult, it is doable if you go about it in the right way and stick to your guns in the process. It is not going to be an overnight process but slow and steady wins the race.

Credit cards: After a foreclosure, many credit card companies will contact you in an attempt to either cancel your account or to raise your rates. Despite what they may say, this is only an automatic adjustment that was triggered based on your foreclosure and is in no way a sure thing. As long as you have been paying your bill on time and are not using the credit card for major purchases, there is no reason you cannot negotiate with the representative that you speak with to both keep your card and keep your rate at the level it was at prior to the foreclosure. Be steadfast in your commitment and don't let them bully you around and you can come out on top.

It is important to keep your credit cards if at all possible as using them is a great way to start reestablishing your credit. You are going to want to use them for household expenses and to pay the charges off in full each month. Maintaining consistency and keeping a clean record of on-time payments is the first step to rebuilding credit.

Secured credit: If you have already lost your credit cards then the easiest way to go about rebuilding your credit is to start with a secured credit card. A secured credit card works like a regular credit card except your limit is tied to the amount of money you deposit with the credit card company up front. You will not be able to access that money directly while the account is open which means the lender doesn't have to worry about losing out on any credit loans that are made in your name.

A secured credit card is different than a debit card in that the company providing it to you will go ahead and make monthly reports to the credit bureaus, helping to build your credit as long as you use it in a conscientious fashion. The card also has all of the fees and penalties of a regular credit card so it is important to shop around for one offers the best rates.

Avoid new debt: When rebuilding your credit, it is important that you don't take on any new debt until your credit score has started to right itself as your debt to income ratio will affect your credit score and, at the moment, you will need all the help you can get. Likewise, starting several new credit streams at once will only shorten the average length of your credit history which can send you back in the other direction. Rather than open new avenues for credit, and debt, focus on paying off any other debts you may current have and save money for when you score gets above 650 so that you can take on new debt with better rates.

Try Low Balance Credit Credits: These credit cards usually have extremely high interest rates but your goal is to charge only 10% of the balance to build a credit score fast. Getting 3-4 of these can achieve excellent results fast if you charge and keep a low (10%) balances on them with no changes. I still have some of my low balance cards that I got just for the purpose of credit repair years ago. For instance I have a $2,000 and $1,000 card. On the $1,000 card I hold a balance of $155 and on the $2,000 card I keep a balance of $180.

Consider credit unions: A credit union is essentially a nonprofit bank that operates only to benefit its members. As such, when you are ready to apply for a new loan or a credit card it is recommended that you join a credit union to do so as the rates that you are eligible for are going to typically be much more in your favor than through a traditional bank. They will also be more likely to overlook your financial mishap as their requirements for loans and credit cards won't be as strict as well.

Chapter 14

FAST CREDIT REPAIR AFTER MEDICAL JUDGMENTS

Unexpected medical expenses can sneak up on anyone at any time with no warning. If a medical judgement is issued against you for costs associated with this type of scenario, the first thing you are going to want to do is to try and fight it using the tactics discussed in chapter 11. If that doesn't work, however, then you are going to have a black mark on your credit report for the next seven years. The most important thing to do in this instance is to not lose hope and to instead do everything you can to repair your credit as quickly as possible.

Negotiate your debt: As previously noted, just because a judgement is filed against you doesn't mean the plaintiff is going to get paid. Medical establishments are aware of this fact which means you can likely negotiate a more reasonable fee as opposed to simply paying what a judge says you owe.

In order to do this, the first thing you are going to need to do is to organize and review your medical bills to ensure they are free of errors including double charges or overcharges. Billing items you can contest include things like full-day charges for the day you were released from the hospital, medication charges and secondary charges for standard supplies such as sheets and gowns as these should be factored into the daily fees. Additionally, if you have insurance you should see a deduction for what they paid on your bill as well.

Once you know exactly what you have to pay, you will then want to compare that amount to your monthly bills and determine how much you can afford to pay of the bill in question. If you only have a small percentage of the total available currently, the best bet is to wait until you have at least fifty percent of the total saved and then reach out to the plaintiff and offer to settle. You can either call the other party or send out the pay for delete letter from chapter 10. Regardless, if you come to an agreement make sure you get it in writing.

Play catchup: If you spent time recuperating from a major illness or accident then it is likely that your medical expenses aren't the only thing you have to deal with, which means the first step to rebuilding your credit is to get your other payments back on track. To do so, you are going to want to contact each of your creditors and explain the situation and ask if you can work out some type of payment plan to get back on track. Generally, you will be able to come to an agreement that you can both live with that won't leave you completely broke. Getting back into the habit of paying all of your bills on time is a crucial step towards rebuilding your credit.

Installment accounts: In addition to opening a secured credit card as described in the previous chapter, you are going to want to go about building positive credit by obtaining an installment loan. This is a loan for a set amount with a set term and a set repayment. Installment loans are easier to get that rotating loans (such as standard credit cards) as the risk to the lender is lessened.

Even still, depending on your current level of credit you may need to get someone who trusts you to cosign on the loan. A cosigner is someone with good credit who essentially gives their word that you are going to pay back the loan, otherwise the failure hurts their credit as well. A good place to look for a starter installment loan is from an independent automotive dealership. These dealers are going to have less stringent requirements than major chains and are often more accustomed to dealing with individuals with less than stellar credit. You may not even need a cosigner after all. If you do get a loan in this fashion, make it a point of always paying the bill on time as this fact will be reported to the credit bureaus on a monthly basis.

Chapter 15

QUICK TECHNIQUES TO REBUILD CREDIT

Pay off what you owe: While this is going to be easier said than done in most situations, according to Experian, the ideal amount of credit utilization that you want is 30 percent or less. While there are other ways to increase your credit utilization rating, paying off what you owe on time each month will also go towards showing you can pay your bills on time, essentially pulling double duty when it comes to improving your credit score. It will also make it easier to follow through on the following tips.

Pay your credit card bills twice a month: If you have a credit card that you use on a regular basis, say for example because it offers you reward points, so much so that you max it out each month, it may actually be hurting your credit even though you pay it off in full at the end of each month. This may be the case due to the way the credit card company reports to the credit bureau; depending on when they report each month it could show that your credit utilization rate is close to 100 percent depending on what your credit line currently is, thus hurting your credit score. As such, paying off your credit card in two smaller chunks throughout the month can actually help boost your credit without costing you anything extra overall.

Increase your credit limit: If you aren't currently in a position to pay down your credit card balance, you can still improve your credit utilization rate by increasing your current credit limit. This is an easy way to improve your credit utilization rate without putting any more money out up front. If you do this, however, it is important that you don't take advantage of the increased credit line as if you find yourself up against the limit again you will be worse off than when you started. Only pursue this option if you have the willpower to avoid racking up extra charges, especially if you are already strapped when it comes to the payments you need to make each month; decreasing your credit utilization limit while also making more late payments is a lateral move at best.

Open a new account: Improving your credit utilization rate is one of the best ways to start rebuilding your credit. If your current credit card company won't increase your credit limit you may way to try applying for another credit card instead. If your credit is not so hot then your rates are going to be higher, but this won't matter as long as you don't plan on using the card in the first place. Remember, credit utilization rate is a combination of your total available lines of credit so this can be a good way to drop your current utilization rate substantially, especially if you won't be able to pay off what you currently owe for a significant period of time.

Keep in mind, however, that if you choose this route then you are only going to want to apply for one new card every couple of months, especially if you aren't sure if you are going to be approved, as too many hard credit inquiries will only cause your credit score to drop, even if you do end up with a better credit utilization rate as a result. Spreading out these requests will give the inquiries time to drop off naturally and will prevent you from looking desperate to potential lenders which can also make it more difficult to get a new card.

Authorized users: If you don't have the credit to get a new credit card, or even to extend your current credit line, then your best choice may be to find someone you trust and ask them to become an authorized user on their card. While most people will likely balk at the idea, you may be able to pacify them by explaining that you don't need a copy of their card or have any intent on using it, simply being listed on the card is enough to improve your credit utilization rating. Not only that, but you will also get credit for the on-time payments that this other person makes as well.

Chapter 16

HOW TO GET LENDER OFFERS

A vast majority of lenders don't have offers that are clearly defined up front, instead they have a general loan package that can be tweaked based on the situation individuals who come to them find themselves in. With this in mind, it becomes apparent why it is so important to seek out multiple offers before making a decision.

Depending on your FICO score, lenders may be more than happy to compete for your business. This fact, coupled with the lack of predetermined rates means that you can easily improve your results by shopping around and then singling out lenders who almost have the rates you are looking for and then telling them that you can get a better deal elsewhere.

To maximize this strategy, you are going to want to make a list of the features you are absolutely going to need to be happy with a given loan and then call each lender you have already talked to and go down the list point by point. If you come across a lender who has an approach that appeals to you, let the other lenders know about it and see what they can do to either match or beat it. They know they are in a competitive business and if you are willing to force their hand they will show you just how much they want your business.

Pre-approved offers: If you took advantage of OptOutPrescreen.com to limit soft inquiries on your credit report and are planning on looking for lenders anytime soon then you may want to reconsider and opt back in, at least for the relatively near future. If you have not opted out of the system, and your credit isn't terrible, then putting in an application with one lender will likely trigger a barrage of competing offers from other lenders as creditors will happily provide your information to anyone and everyone who is interested in selling you on their services.

While this can be annoying in some cases, if you are looking for the best lender possible then it could be just what you need to pit several lenders against one another. Prescreened offers can make it easier for you to compare relative costs or special offers as long as you do your due diligence with each and ensure that you aren't being hornswoggled by smoke and mirrors.

Ensure you have a loan estimate document: The loan estimate document was created by the Consumer Financial Protection Bureau to make it easier for borrowers to compare the various costs associated with individual loans and lenders. Its job is to standardize and simplify the way that lenders expose their fees so that you aren't comparing apples to oranges. The loan estimate document can be downloaded from ConsumerFinance.gov.

In addition to make it easier to compare various potential loans, it makes it easy to be aware of the various fees that are sure to pile up along the way, even with the most apparently straightforward of loans. It also breaks down costs in a way that anyone can understand without the help of a CPA. It includes all sorts of useful information including estimated monthly payments, prepayment penalties and the interest rate of the various loans in question.

Lock in the best rate: Once you have done the work of comparing the various options available to you, the next thing you are going to want to do is to ensure that the best option doesn't change while you are making all of the relevant arrangements. To ensure this is the case you are going to want to ask the lender for a written rate lock or lock-in. This is a written and legally binding guarantee that the lender will give you the interest rate you discussed for the price you discussed for a set period of time. It protects you from interest rate increases that may occur while your loan is being processed. It is important to keep in mind that some lenders will charge for a lock-in while others will not it all depends on the individual lender.

Chapter 17

HOW TO BUILD BUSINESS CREDIT

Approximately 45 percent of all small businesses who are turned down for a loan have bad credit to blame, according to the Federal Reserve Banks of Philadelphia, Cleveland, Atlanta and New York. A robust credit profile for your business doesn't just make it easier to get a loan, it will also make it easier for your business to attract new customers. This is because, unlike with your personal credit report, anyone including potential suppliers, partners and customers can all see the credit report of your business at any time. With this fact in mind, it should be clear that if you own a small business, you will want to do everything in your power to improve its credit as quickly as possible and keep it clean as well.

Know your current score: While you are already familiar with Equifax and Experian, when it comes to keeping tabs on your business credit score you are also going to need to familiarize yourself with the Dun & Bradstreet credit bureau. Unfortunately, while determining your personal credit score is relatively straightforward, all three bureaus use a different means of determining business credit scores as well as asking various lenders for differing types of data. This will sometimes work to your advantage, however as Dun & Bradstreet lets business owners update their basic business details and also upload financial data. Even better complete portfolios actually improving overall credit scores.

Set up trade lines: Assuming you purchase materials from third-party vendors, doing so in the right way can help you to improve your business' credit. Assuming you have been

66

working with a given vendor for some time, it is likely that they would be willing to extend you trade credit for the things you purchase most often. Trade credit simply means that you will be able to pay a predetermined number of weeks, or even just days, after you have received the latest shipment of inventory. Once you set up this type of relationship it is then easy to ask the supplier to report your payments to the relevant credit bureaus.

You will want to try your hardest to establish at least three of these types of relationships as doing so will allow you to get what is known as a Paydex score through Dun & Bradstreet which is a measure of your successful payment history. Even if you form relationships with smaller vendors who don't typically report details, by listing them on your account as trade references the bureau will then follow up with them to generate your score.

Be prompt with payments: Just like with your personal finances, paying creditors on time is a crucial part of building your business credit successfully. If you are looking to get the best Paydex score from Dun & Bradstreet you are going to need to go above and beyond and make all your payments early, no exceptions. Additionally, the longer your credit history the better so the sooner you can start forming these relationships the better it will be for your score.

Borrow from the right lenders: While having a loan and paying it on time can help to boost your business' credit score, this will only be the case if the lender you choose reports to the bureaus which is far from guaranteed. Do your homework and make sure that your fiscal responsibility is helping you out as much as possible when you do get a loan. Most banks will report to the bureaus as do the online lenders including

BlueVine, Kabbage, Funding Circle Fundation, Lending Club and OnDeck. Fundbox, Lighter Captial, SmarBiz and most merchant cash advance companies do not. If you are using business credit cards, strive to keep your credit utilization under 20 percent for the best results.

Be aware of your public records: Just like your business credit report, your public records can also be seen by anyone which means you are going to want to do your best to stay on the right side the law. Not only will negative public records affect your business credit score, they will affect the way the public perceives your business as well.

Chapter 18

STOP COLLECTORS FAST

While it is always going to be a better choice to deal with creditors directly rather than waiting for a debt to reach collections, if it does reach this point it is important to keep in mind that you still have options thanks to what is known as the Fair Debt Collection Practices act.

Ask for details in writing: Within 5 days of making contact, a debt collector is obligated to send you a written notice outlining the amount of money you owe, who you owe it to and how to dispute the claim. Most debt collectors won't do this automatically, however which means the first contact you have with them should include asking for this information and nothing else. The goal of the debt collector is to force you to confirm that you will pay the debt or make a payment, and not having all of the details in front of you can make it easy to say the wrong thing and wave many of your rights without even realizing it. What's more, asking for a copy of the details will prevent them from contacting you again until you have received them, giving you some time to get your defenses together if you have been caught off guard.

Dispute the claim: Once you have received the details of the claim in writing, the next thing you are going to want to do is to dispute the claim using the methods discussed in previous chapters, regardless of whether or not you believe you owe the money in question. This will put the onus on the collection agency to verify the debt, which is far from a sure thing even on debts that you do owe. You have 30 days to send this letter from the date you received the details which means that using certified mail is key. Be sure to ask for a delivery receipt as nine times out of ten the collections agency will deny they received your request. Once you send this letter and notify the collection agency of this fact, they cannot contact you again until the debt has been verified. **They also have to stop all reporting activity, make sure you demand this in the letter.**

Keep track of everything: As discussed previously, debt collectors are limited in how they can approach you but, in most cases, will try and skirt these restrictions as much as possible in an effort to get you to agree to pay the debt or set up a payment plan. As such, it is in your best interest to take detailed notes every time you speak with them and keep anything they send you so you can look it over for violations at a later date.

Illegal activities not previously covered include speaking to anyone but you or your representation about the debt, using abusive language, misrepresenting the amount of the debt of making false claims about legal action, seizing property or garnishing wages if they don't intend to actually follow through. If they do any of these things, then the issue of the amount of debt you owe will essentially become moot as you will be able to take legal action against them and even the threat of doing so will often be enough for them to forgive some or all of your debt entirely. Be sure not to mention that you are keeping track of your conversations as this will cause them to be on their best behavior and decrease your potential for leverage.

Speak as little as possible: Everything that a debt collector says is for the purpose of collecting on the debt which means that the less you say, the less they have to use against you. Remember, regardless of what they may say up front, they are never really your friend, nor do they have your best interests at heart. They work on commission which means the more they get from you the more they will make. Never commit to anything, never agree that you owe the amount in question, always mention that you are considering bankruptcy and discuss payment options only if you intend to follow through. If they determine that you are unlikely to pay, and the amount owed is less than $2,500, they may give up and consider you more trouble than you are worth. While the debt will remain on your credit report for the next seven years, it might be worth it, depending on your current financial situation.

Be aware of time limits: Once you receive the details from the collection agency, you will need to look into the timeframe which they have to collect on the debt based on where you live (between three and six years in most cases). Once this period of time has passed they can no longer take legal action against you. It is important to be aware of these limits as if you make a payment after this period of time, some states will allow the clock to be reset, the same can be said for acknowledging you owe the debt or for signing up for a repayment plan.

Chapter 19

HOW TO NEGOTIATE AND SETTLE LARGE DEBTS

While creditors would like you to think otherwise, the fact of the matter is that any debt that you have is negotiable. What's more, regardless of the amount, 90 percent of creditors are going to be willing to take a lump sum now over a promise to pay at a later date. When it comes to negotiating large amounts, the following tips may make it easier to come out ahead.

Have a story and stick with it: The person you are dealing with isn't going to be interested in your life story, but they will need to know why you are unable to pay in full right now. This means you are going to want to have a story that outlines your hardships and explains what you are doing to get back on track. You will want to distill that story down to the most important points and never waver from it throughout the negotiation process.

One particularly useful strategy is mentioning that, due to financial hardship, you will soon be meeting with a lawyer who specializes in bankruptcy. This will almost always make creditors more willing to strike a deal as if you file for bankruptcy there is a chance that they will get nothing.

Stay calm: It is important to keep in mind that, no matter what the creditor says, you have the upper hand as the debt you have is leverage over them. Stick to this fact and, no matter what they say, do your best to avoid losing your temper. If you make a scene or cause drama then the creditor will know they are getting to you and will be less willing to make a deal. If you feel yourself losing it, simply tell them that you will call them back and end the call as quickly as possible. If you find the creditor's behavior hard to stomach, simply tell them you are recording the conversation which will put them on their best, and most professional, behavior.

Always ask questions: If the creditor threatens you with a lawsuit or with the loss of property, above all else it is important that you don't let these threats frighten you into making a poor decision. Instead, it is important to ask questions as this will often reveal if the creditor is bluffing or not. For example, if they threaten you with a lawsuit, simply ask when you can expect to be notified of it. Keep notes of these threats as they are often times illegal as creditors are strictly limited as to how they can approach debt, specifically to protect consumers.

Likewise, you are going to want to take notes every time you speak with a creditor including the name of the person you spoke with, the date and the things that were discussed, especially threats. There is typically a statute of limitations as to how long the creditor has to collect on a debt, which varies by region, and they will likely become irater as that time period approaches.

Avoid agreeing to a payment plan: If you agree to a payment plan you will always end up paying more in the long run then if you manage to scrape together a lump sum payment. Depending on the amount you owe, even as little as 30 percent might be enough to satisfy the creditor assuming it is getting close to the end of the timeframe they have to collect on the debt and you have stuck to your story about financial hardship and bankruptcy. Never be afraid to offer a lowball number, the worst that can happen is that they refuse to take it. If you do end up agreeing to a payment plan make sure you go over your expenses with a fine-tooth comb and ensure you can afford to make the payment every month to avoid finding yourself back in the same situation.

Try and deal with creditors: If you know you are going to be unable to make payments on a debt you have accrued, do your best to come to an agreement with the creditor directly, before the debt is sent to collections. The creditor is always going to be easier to negotiate with than a third-party debt collection service.

Chapter 20

MAINTAINING YOUR CREDIT

Once you have done the work of repairing your damaged credit score you are going to want to do everything in your power in order to ensure that you don't find yourself back where you started. You have worked diligently to repair the mistakes of the past; don't use it as an excuse to start making new ones. To help keep you on the straight and narrow, consider the following tips.

Always pay your bills on time, all of them: While not every bill that you have will end up on your credit report if you are a few days late when it comes to paying it, you can never know for certain which bills are mission critical and which can be safely ignored until your next pay check. Even a small fine from the local library could ultimately end up on your credit report, dinging your hard-won credit score in the process. Don't take that chance and always remain vigilant when it comes to paying your bills on time.

Avoid using credit cards: While having credit cards improves your credit utilization and credit history, using them too often is a surefire way to start back-sliding, especially if your budget is on the lean side. If you must use your credit cards, take special care to ensure that you never exceed a credit utilization of 30 percent as that's when your credit score will start to take a hit. While going over this limit slightly will only affect your score by a few points, if you are just on the edge of an acceptable score, that might be all it takes to start seeing higher rates as a result.

Pay down your loans: Once you have righted your financial ship, the best way you can keep it on course is to make it a point of paying down your loans as quickly as possible; don't forget, approximately 30 percent of your credit score is influenced by the amount of debt you have which makes it one of the easiest ways to continue improving your score once you are moving in the right direction.

In order to make more money available to pay down your debt, the first thing you are going to want to do is to stop living paycheck to paycheck which means establishing an emergency fund. A solid emergency fund will allow you to live for three months, and pay all your bills, if the worst happens and you find yourself out of the job. Establishing this fund will give you the wiggle room you need to prioritize your debt without worrying about every minor pitfall that comes your way.

Monitor spending: Approximately 40 percent of individuals who find themselves with credit score issues got there simply by not keeping track of their week-to-week spending as well as they should. With the prevalence of online banking, there is no reason why you shouldn't be aware of exactly what your checking account balance is, every minute of every day. Get in the habit of monitoring your spending and you will never be surprised when your bank statement shows up at the end of the month. This doesn't mean you won't want to peruse the statement when it does come in, however, as you never know when a mistake might be made, you never know when a little extra diligence could pay off in a big way.

Remain glued to your credit report: Just because you are out of the woods doesn't mean that nothing new is going to show up on your credit report, whether it is your fault or not. Something new from your past might show up, or one of the bureaus may make a mistake or fail to note the positive changes you have made in a timely manner. The previous chapters have given you tools for dealing with these issues, but you will only be able to put them into action if you are aware of them in the first place. Don't let all your hard work go to waste, continue taking advantage of your free credit report every year.

Chapter 21

FRAUD AND IDENTITY THEFT PREVENTION

Once you have established a quality credit score, you need to do your best to protect it by taking extra steps to prevent identity theft and other types of fraud. The following tips will help you do so:

Respond to voicemail intelligently: If you receive a voicemail from someone claiming to be from your credit card company or bank, only respond by calling back the number that is printed on your card. This is the only number you can guarantee won't lead to a fraud scenario. The same goes for emails, even if they appear to be legitimate, you should only ever contact your bank or credit card company through obviously official channels that you instigate to ensure they are legitimate.

Take extra care with signatures: Not many people are aware, but you can actually sign your credit and debit cards with the phrase "see identification". While this will force you to show your ID much more frequently, it will also prevent anyone who is attempting to use it illegally from being able to do so. Unless they have a fake ID with your name and accurate signature they will be out of luck.

Be frugal with your credit card number: Ninety percent of the time any website that asks for your credit or debit card number "for identification purposes" has only dubious intentions in mind. Unless you are planning on buying something from the site you are going to want to avoid providing this information.

The fewer places that your personal details are available online the less risk you run of falling victim to fraud.

Be diligent about your privacy: Even if you have already set them to the max settings, it is important to check both your browser and social media settings on a regular basis to ensure they are as you left them. You never know when an update could have come along and reset them or changed something else that affected them in some way. It only takes one slip to allow someone with malicious intent through, which is why it pays to stay vigilant. Likewise, every time you visit a secure website, take an extra moment to clear your browser's cache and history to prevent anyone from tracking down personal information that way.

Unsubscribe sparingly: If you receive an email newsletter and you aren't sure where it came from, never click the unsubscribe button. This will let the spammer know that they have a live email address and they will redouble their efforts, at best, or initiate additional tactics to procure your private data now that they have your email address, at worst. Even if the spammer has no ulterior motives than to get you to read their newsletter you are always better off just hitting the spam button and forgetting about it.

Be aware of online store security: When you are shopping online be sure to make a point of never entering sensitive information if the website isn't secure. You can determine if a site is using a secure connection if the web address starts with http**s** or if it features a padlock icon in the top right corner. Either of these are an indicator that the website is encrypted which will make it much more difficult for fraud to occur based on the transaction. Entering your details via a standard http connection is little more than asking for trouble.

Have varying passwords: In addition to the obvious, such as not using birthdays or loved ones' names as passwords, it is important to have varying levels of password security for the most secure results. You are going to want to have at least one password for low-security sites that you aren't terribly worried about being hacked, a more secure password for online stores and the like and a separate password entirely when it comes to banks or credit card websites that are more complicated still. You should never store your passwords anywhere on your computer or anywhere in real life where other people, with potentially malicious intent, are likely to have access to and, if you must write them down, don't keep them near your computer.

Cyber Threats & Privacy

Identity theft and hacking are growing at super exponential rates. It won't stop and will only get worse. The fact is that most Americans are already compromised and they don't even know it. It is estimated that over 80% of all residential households in American do not even have their WiFi router secured properly.

Identity theft, which leads to ruined credit and finances, often starts with a hidden cyber breach, which can happen anywhere, your home devices, you mobile phone, or a third party vendor that stores your credit card in their ecommerce database. Do not rely on third parties like LifeLock to protect you, think about how important this is.

Basic Mandatory Cyber Security

Secure your home WiFi router: Secure your home router by making a long complex PSK password, get rid of any default settings and TURN OFF WPS (Wireless Protected Setup). Also set your WiFi router to WPA2/CCMP-AES mode as it is the current highest security setting available on most routers. Also ensure your non-WiFi router has a basic firewall and that all options are on. Try to only do financial log-ins and transactions on your WIRED computer/network instead of WiFi.

Encrypt your phone and computers: These encryptions are nearly impossible to break. This is a good safety feature in case your computer or mobile device is lost/stolen.

Use A VPN (Virtual Private Network): There are many vendors to choose from that will give you continuous coverage on multiple devices for a nominal fee. Be sure to only use a vendor that uses the **OpenVPN protocol**, currently the most secure tunneling protocol. We recommend ProtonVPN or ExpressVPN.

Secure website browsing: Be sure your browser uses the HTTPS protocol, or only visits site with the HTTPS certificate validated (SSL/TLS protocols)

Beware of email phishing scam: These are the most common hacks because they take advantage of people's psychology. These emails look authentic and trick many people into thinking they are logging into their bank or credit card company. The outcome is obvious, the email is fake and was set up to capture your credentials. It's best to not even respond to an email ever asking for your username, password or any personal information. Check the email headers to see where the it's really coming from.

Wireless Card Scanners (NFC hackers)

These are hackers that will scan your credit card in your pocket at coffee shops or other unassuming public places. They have special devices or programs that can "see" the RF chips embedded in your credit card on their laptops, in close ranges. This happened to me once but since I was set up on **banking text alerts** I was able to stop it and get my money back. I now use radio frequency shield card slots and wallets to prevent this from happening again, which you can buy on Amazon.

Online Banking

Make sure your network is secure and the browser is set to HTTPS when logging into your banking account. One small compromise and someone can steal your info, and ruin your credit. In fact any website you submit personal info on should start with HTTPS (Secure) URL.

As stated previously, over 80% of all U.S. homes do not secure their wifi router. Most people never change their factory default router login and password. Any hacker that scans your neighborhood (anyone can do this with a mobile phone now and a Wi-Fi app) can generally determine what kind of router model you have from the SSID default broadcast, and then check to see if they can login using the default pass and username.

If a hacker is able to break into your home network, you can have some serious compromises. This often leads to cases of identity theft and fraud. Most often you will not know about it until well after the compromise has occurred and someone has used your information to steal money or your identity.

The cyber threats are very real and much worse than you think; they are only getting more complex everyday as hackers develop new technologies and methods to scan for weaknesses and infiltrate unassuming homes, people and businesses.

Shred your mail, bills or paperwork that may have sensitive personal info on them. You would be surprised to know that people still rummage through garbage to find data to sell or use for gain.

Use Secured Email

Almost everyone sends sensitive info via email and text not even thinking that someone can scan that data in "cyberspace" if they are looking for it. Since most people are now using Gmail,Yahoo Hotmail, etc. There aren't very many secure options for email if you are not using Thunderbird or Outlook. Out of the free email account, Gmail is the most secure. **However, there is one company in Switzerland that has a service called ProtonMail.com.**

It a browser email account with mobile phone apps that send and received encrypted mail and is very easy to use. They have a free account version and a paid account version, which is approximately $6 per month. If you send personal data via email such as tax returns, social security numbers, credit card numbers... Check out ProtonMail.com

Commercial Mailbox

Use a commercial mail box, such as the UPS store mail box, for receiving your postal mail instead of receiving it at home. UPS Stores are very flexible and can even forward your mail wherever you are. Many thieves still steal mail in an attempt to find social security numbers, checks, or anything they can use to extract money or credit from a victim.

Conclusion

Just because you've finished this book doesn't mean there is nothing left to learn on the topic, expanding your horizons is the only way to find the mastery you seek. While laws regarding these issues are fairly set in stone, the credit bureaus are always petitioning the federal government to update the FCRA to focus on electronic forms of communication which means looking up the latest rulings is always encouraged.

The next step is to stop reading already and to get ready to get started rebuilding your credit as quickly and effectively as possible. While you are certainly facing an uphill battle, it is important to keep in mind that it is far from unwinnable, and the information discussed in the preceding chapters will go a long way towards making your fight a lot more manageable. Above all, it is important to keep in mind that repairing your credit is a marathon, not a sprint which means that slow and steady wins the race. Make a plan, stick with it, and you will be able to improve your credit score by 100 points or more sooner than you may think.

If you found this book useful in anyway,
a review on Amazon is always appreciated!

Book Two

Credit Repair

Remove Negative Accounts and Increase Your Score Quickly By Using Federal Laws That Favor You.

<u>BONUS:</u>

<u>Actual Real Life Credit Disputes Included.</u>

Table of Contents

Author's Message 89

Chapter 1: Introduction to Credit 92

Chapter 2: Your Credit 99

Chapter 3: How to Understand and Monitor Your Credit

    Score 111

Chapter 4: Your Rights..123

Chapter 5: How to Remove Negative Records.....................136

Chapter 6: Correspondence Letter Templates.................... 149

Chapter 7: Preventing Fraud.. 160

Author's Message

Credit..The American Way?

Yes, I used to be a guy with CRAP credit, a 409 credit score, several collection accounts, public judgments, garnishments and the only people that ever called me were creditors, they were my best friends. I probably sound like a real bum deadbeat to you, right? I certainly felt like it, I was rejected for apartments, home loans, car loans, jobs, you name it, and it sucked!

I couldn't even open a bank account because I was placed into the "CHEX" system they use for people that over-drafted an account and never paid it off.

For years I had to cash my check at "Ace Check Cashing" stores in Cleveland, Ohio! So was I really a dead beat and bum?

Not really, I had my own apartment and a $50,000 a year job when this all went down, and this was when $50,000 a year actually paid the bills, it was a great secure job I worked really hard to get, but I made a few bad decisions with my credit, and had some high medical bills from minor medical problems I had suddenly (before the job). But, there was no mercy, when I was unable to pay them; the creditors used the harshest, most vicious methods to get money from me, by garnishing my wages.

I let them roll right over me at age 23, and roll they did, they destroyed my finances, took my money, ruined my credit and basically did whatever the hell they could get away with, and believe me, THEY KNOW WHAT THEY ARE DOING, they enjoy it, they have a "ME vs. YOU" mentality, you KNOW WHY?

BECAUSE "THEY" JUST WANT YOUR MONEY, AND THEY WILL DO ANYTHING TO GET IT, EVEN BREAKING THE CONSUMER LAWS TO GET IT BECAUSE THE PROVEN AVERAGES ARE THAT less than .5% of American consumers will fight back and defend their rights!

When I started my fight, I won initially, but the thing is, many creditors will hire law firms to collect debt, of which individual accounts may be handled by individual attorneys **that LOVE messing with you**, they will go out of their way to really drive the stake into you, **because it makes them look good**, it's a game to them and it satisfies their **huge ego** (most collections lawyers have the largest egos out of all professions, search for any stats and you will see this is true).

So when I won my case against a garnishment, the attorney handling my collections for the creditor found a loophole to garnish me for an additional $32 unpaid service fee they found with the same client-creditor, he immediately (next day) filed for garnishment of this plus all legal costs($500) the next DAY, and he got it. FYI, this law firm was "Javitch, Block and Rathbone", in Cleveland, OH. They are no longer in business.

You see, we live in a system that is a game, it's a money grab, and the way business and digital transactions are escalating online is making it easier for large corporations, banks and credit card companies to get away with more, because they know that YOU the consumer or borrower will not have the time or energy to fight back, because you are too busy with your job and life. Seriously, isn't this true? It takes time to fight back, unless you hire a lawyer, but why pay a lawyer when a couple well-well-written strategic demand letters can get you very far.

It's truly a biased credit world, but there is hope, and it starts with you learning how to fight back and protect YOUR credit report. It isn't hard; you just need to know what to do and where to get the information the federal government has made available to anyone that wants to defend their rights using the Fair Credit Acts. A few written certified letters can literally change your entire destiny, it did for me, and it could for you.

If there is ONE THING you get from this short book, it is to not follow the traditional online route of credit dispute, that's what the rest of the millions of credit disputers are doing. If you really take this seriously and want real results or attention, write some really good damn letters to the PEOPLE THAT MATTER. For instance, why write a letter to a bank's "credit dispute department" when you can get it in front of the CEO and President with a little work? How about the statutory agent for the corporations? They are obligated to forward all mail directly to the company's legal team and decision makers. All of this info is online, there is no excuse, and you have to do these things to fight for your credit report. So , very important, write good, concise, factual, well-thought letters making your case and make sure you get it to one or several authority/decision makers in the company (creditor).

Chapter 1

Introduction to Credit

The American Credit Rating Systems

Explanation of Common Credit-Related Terms

Before you start reading this book, you should read through the definitions in the list below. They are the list of terms that will be commonly used throughout the text. You might know what some of these terms are, but this information is presented to prepare you for continued reading even if you have no prior knowledge regarding credit.

- Credit: Credit can mean a host of things but for the context of this book, it means an amount that has been lent to you by a lender such as a bank with the expectation that you will pay back the amount plus interest in a timely manner.
- Credit Report: Your credit report is the compiled record of your credit history that is used in credit decisions. It will include your personal details like birth date, address etc. It will also have information about your existing credit which includes any open accounts like credit cards, mortgages, and student and car loans. It will have the terms and how well you paid on those terms as well. Some information from your public record will also be on your credit reports such as any court judgments, bankruptcies, and tax liens you may have against you. Lastly, it will have information on inquiries into your credit.

- Credit Score: A credit score is a document that allows lenders to predict your likelihood of repaying debts. Your credit score is different yet related to your credit report since it is calculated using the information in your report. Some important things are to be considered when viewing your credit score. These include how many and what types of credit accounts you have or have had in the past, how well you have paid your bills on time, or if you have collections against you or other outstanding debt. This is also called a credit rating.

- Consumer: A consumer is someone who is involved in the economy by purchasing goods and services for their personal use. In credit, this term is used to refer to anyone who has a credit report or has credit issued to them by a creditor.

- Creditor: A creditor is a company that furnishes information for consumer reporting agencies about consumers that have a credit agreement with them. These companies include mortgage banking institutions and credit card and auto finance companies.

- Consumer Reporting Agency (CRA): A CRA is are any person or business that assembles information on consumers and sells or otherwise engages in disseminating that information for preparing or furnishing consumer reports.

- Credit Bureau: A credit bureau is a type of consumer reporting agency (CRA) that gathers information from creditors and then disseminates that information for use in making credit decisions. The information is also used for some other purposes such as employment.

- Tax Lien: Tax liens are legal remedies that your creditors can use to collect payment for your debts from you. If you have a tax lien against you, the IRS has a legal right to your property such as you home, bank accounts, or car.

- Charge-off: Charge-offs occur when you are very late paying on a debt account. Usually, a charge-off will show up on your credit report after you have not paid on your account for over 180 days. A charge-off means that your creditor has decided that the money you owe is not collectible and will write it off as a tax loss. Even if this occurs, you are still liable for the debt.

- Judgements: A judgment is a public record that will show up on your credit report if a court has ruled against you and thus you owe money on a lawsuit. This can happen for a variety of reasons such as unpaid collections. Since judgements are public records, they can be seen by anyone who searches for the information and is easily discovered and collected by credit bureaus for your credit report.

How to Use This Book:

This book was written with an audience in the United States of America because laws and procedures are different in every country. Despite this, many people around the world may still find some of the information presented in the following chapters to be useful.

There is a lot of information packed into this book. For that reason, you should be aware of what is contained in each chapter so that you can find exactly what information is most relevant to your needs at any time.

Chapter two, Your Credit, will explain what your credit is used for, what a credit bureau is and how they operate, where they get your information, and how it is used. It will also explain what is in a credit report and how to read one and present a list of information you are likely to find in a credit report.

Chapter three, How to Understand and Monitor Your Credit Score, will explain the different types of types of credit scores going into depth on the most common???, the FICO scoring system and how it is calculated. It will also tell you what a good credit score is and why, how credit scoring can actually help you, and how to monitor your credit online.

Chapter four, Your Rights, will explain what you are entitled to under the Fair Credit Reporting Act (FCRA), what other rights you may have in your state, and what federal question jurisdiction is and how it can be used in your favor.

Chapter five, How to Remove Negative Records, will explain different ways to remove things from your credit report that harm your credit score. You will read about removing late payment notices, charge-offs, collections, judgments, and tax liens as well as when to use cease and desist letters for debt collectors and the dangers of using online correspondence to deal with your credit report.

Chapter six, Correspondence Letter Templates, will explain how to write dispute letters, cease and desist letters, and goodwill letters, as well as provide you with templates to guide your writing.

Chapter seven, Preventing Fraud, will cover how consumer information is stored, secured, and used, what data brokers are and how they operate, what identity theft is, how it happens, and what to do about it, how to protect yourself online, and how to place a credit freeze or fraud alert on your credit report. This chapter is especially important to protecting yourself before negative situations can occur.

Chapter eight, More Things You Should Know, will teach you how to opt-out of data brokers, use United States Postal Service (USPS) tracking, why you should use a commercial mail receiving agency, and how to settle medical debt.

Immigrant's Credit

If you are an immigrant to the United States, you should know that your credit history will be affected by that fact. Every country keeps track of their citizen's credit history independently. Thus your credit history will usually stay in your country of origin. This is applicable even on credit cards that operate within a multinational credit bureau. A good example would be Equifax. They do not share information with Equifax Canada.

Therefore, if you move to the United States you will typically not have any credit history for a credit report or score. This makes it difficult to qualify for housing, auto loans, insurance, or credit cards even if you have a good score in your country of origin. This problem can work in reverse and arise when American citizens move to another country as well.

Rarely, lenders will take credit history from another country into account when approving credit. One such company is American Express. They can transfer a credit card from country to country which can help when building a new credit history in a new country. When you move with a credit card like that, you start with a good credit record right away as long as you have good history with the card.

If you do not have a line of credit that can be moved from a different country, it may be necessary to work for several years before you can qualify for a credit card or mortgage.

How to Build a Credit History:

To have a credit score, and therefore qualify for many more opportunities that require credit, you need to have at least one account that is six months old or older and has been reported to the credit bureaus for the previous six months. There are a lot of opportunities for people without a credit history or with bad credit history to build credit.

The first method is to apply for a secured credit card. What is a secured credit card? It is a line of credit that you open with a cash deposit. The deposit you will need to open the account is usually the limit of your credit. Other than the deposit, the card will work like any other credit card except the deposit is kept for collateral if you do not pay your balance. If you do not miss payments and close the account, you will receive your deposit back. Usually, this type of credit is meant to be temporary so that you can qualify for other types of credit that will not require a deposit.

The next step you can take is to apply for a credit-builder loan. This type of loan is only for building credit. Usually the money you "borrow" is held by your lender until you pay it back. Basically, it is forcing you to pay into a savings account of sorts. However, just as with any loan, the fact that you are making regular payments is reported to the credit bureaus. You can usually apply at credit unions and community banks.

Another route you can take is to open a loan or unsecured credit card with the help of a co-signer. The co-signer is typically someone you know, like a parent that has a good credit history and the ability to pay your debt if you cannot. It is an assurance to the creditor that they will be repaid since they do not yet know if they can trust you.

In the same vein, you can also be listed as an authorized user on someone else's line of credit. A family member or significant other might allow you to get a credit card linked to their account. This gives you the privileges of having a credit card and credit history reported to credit bureaus on your behalf without needing to qualify on your own. Be sure to pay your share of the debt if asked as even though you will not be legally obligated the person can remove you from the account if you break their trust.

Another way to build credit is to use a rent-reporting service. Companies like Rental Kharma and RentTrack will take a bill you are paying and report it to the credit bureaus. Although not every score will utilize this type of history, it will still look good to lenders.

Once you start to build or rebuild your credit, make sure to keep your score up by using good practices. Avoid missed or late payments at all cost even on things like utilities. Keep a credit to debt ratio as low as possible (30% is recommended), do not open several accounts at one time, keep unused accounts open unless they have fees to improve your credit to debt ratio and account age, and check all of your credit reports every year.

Chapter 2

Your Credit

You are your credit. That might sound like an exaggeration, but both your credit report and credit score have the power to heavily affect nearly every aspect of your life. Getting an apartment on mortgage, a bank account or credit card, or a personal or business loan will be affected. If your score is low, you will have a higher interest rate or might not be able to get what you are applying for at all. Even signing up for utilities and services such as telephone, internet, or television could be affected. Insurance companies can also look at your credit history to set the rates and premiums you will have to pay.

Potential employers may even look at your credit history which could cost you a possible job. It has been estimated that one quarter of Americans that are unemployed had to have their credit checked when applying to one or more jobs. Due to this concerning??? fact, it is a federal regulation that an employer must receive permission from a candidate to check their credit. This is still not an ideal situation.

As you can see, there is no way around it. You have to have at least a decent credit score to be able to succeed in today's world. If your score is too bad, you might have trouble finding housing, insurance, important services and utilities, and even holding a job. Even a slightly bad score could mean you get bad interest rates which could mean thousands of extra dollars down the drain over the years, especially in the case of a mortgage or car payment.

To understand your credit better, you need to learn about the credit bureau, where your credit history comes from, and how to read your credit report.

What Is A Credit Bureau, Where Do They Get My Information, And How Is It Used?

A credit bureau, sometimes also called a credit reporting agency (CRA), is a profit-making company that collects the information about you that is related to your credit report and makes it available to the companies and banks. They, in turn, use it to make decisions about your ability and willingness to pay for something. There are three of these companies that are the most used: Equifax, Experian, and TransUnion. Generally, these are the three credit reports that are used when determining things like mortgage rates and your overall credit scores.

Each of these reports is going to be slightly different since each service or lender that reports information on your credit will choose which of these companies to report to. Sometimes, a lender, bank, finance company, or utility company will only report to one or sometimes they will report to all three. Sometimes, they do not report to any bureau. This means if you want to build or repair your credit, make sure the service you are using reports your information.

Your credit report is also affected by public records. These include records such as court or property records such as legal judgements, bankruptcy, or foreclosure. These records may also be different between the three reports as the different credit bureaus get their information from different sources here as well.

Credit bureaus ability to gain all this information about millions of people has made them databases that are somewhat like warehouses of information due to their size. The information they gather is compiled into your credit report, through which your credit score is generated. What they do with this information is largely up to who they sell the data to, as will be explained below.

When you apply for something that requires a credit report or score, you fill out an application form that requests your details like social security number. Then, this information is forwarded to the credit bureau where they match the provided information with the information on file. When the lender, utility service, bank, or whatever else needs that information receives it, they are the ones to decide how credit-worthy you are.

Yes, it actually is not the credit bureau that decides if you get that loan or are allowed to sign up for a television service, it is each individual lender or company. The bureau simply gathers your data and sells it to whoever wants it. This means the cut-off point of both willingness to repay and ability to repay (wages) is different for each situation. Every time you need to use your credit, there are different requirements that you need to meet and most of the time these are not disclosed to you before or after you apply. The only exception to this is if you are denied, then the reason must be disclosed.

There are a lot of people that can see the information collected by credit bureaus as well. Even though access is limited to those with legitimate business or legal reasons, what constitutes a legitimate use is far-reaching. Lenders who are being requested by you, have already given you credit, and those which want to offer you credit can all gain access. Also, as mentioned already, telephone and other utility companies, employers, and insurance companies (both those you have applied for and those that want to offer you their service) can all gain access as well. Additionally, landlords, banks you are opening a checking account at, and government agencies that decide if you qualify for benefits are allowed your credit information as well. Your records can be subpoenaed in a court of law too. That is quite a long list of people who have access to personal identifying information and can make decisions that can mean the difference between being employed with a roof over your head or not based on that information.

To make matters worse, any negative information you have on that report stays there for at least seven years, or sometimes longer. Things like late or missed payments, criminal convictions, liens, and wage garnishment stay on your record for seven years' minimum. A bankruptcy stays for ten years.

Your Credit Report Explained

First of all, to understand your credit report, you need to see one. Everyone is entitled to a free credit report prepared by reputable companies like Equifax, Experian, and TransUnion- every year. You can get all of the reports at once or spread them out. This will largely depend on what you want to do with the reports. If you want to see everything there is on your credit at once, get all three. If you want to monitor changes over time, it is recommended to spread them out and request one every four months. Be sure to note when you get your reports so that you can get them again the next year.

Getting your credit report is fairly simple, especially for the free ones. Just visiting our website or calling us and providing the required details will allow you to see your report. You might also be requested to provide some details which you will probably need your records for. A typical question might be asking which of four choices (one of which will be "none of the above") did you use to open a line of credit in 2014. Online, it is instantaneous, whereas you must wait for it to come in the mail if you call.

If you want to see your credit report more often, you will have to pay to access it unless it is one of a few specific instances. This will be about twenty dollars.

To see your credit score, it is a bit different but goes hand in hand with your report and what effects it has on your life. Monitoring your score will be covered in more detail later in this book so we will not cover it too much here. However, you usually receive a free score when applying for credit such as for a personal or business loan, credit card, mortgage, or car loan. If you wish to see your credit score, you usually have to purchase it from one of the credit bureaus. There are ways to view free credit scores online but most are "thin" as they do not go as deep or use as much information as full score from a legitimate company. That is not to say that these scores cannot be useful for regular tracking but be sure to see your true score at least a few times year.

If you want to purchase your score from a major company, visit their websites or call their number.

Equifax: Call 1-800-685-1111 or visit
https://www.equifax.com/personal/

Experian: Call 1-888-397-3742 or visit
https://www.experian.com/consumer-products/credit-score.html

TransUnion: Call 1-800-493-2392 or visit
https://www.transunion.com/

If you find that you have adverse credit, which is often called non-status credit history, poor credit history, sub-prime credit history, bad credit history or impaired credit history, it means you have a negative credit rating. This is a negative when applying for loans and other services.

How to Read a Credit Report

Now that you know the basics about what your credit report is, how to get it, and what it does for you, you need to learn how to navigate and understand the information it provides. To start off, there are probably several things on your report that you will not understand. That is okay. This section will walk you through exactly how to read your credit report.

If this is the first time you have looked at your reports or you have not seen them in over a year, you should probably go through the steps explained in the last section and get all three of the major credit bureaus reports at once so you can understand the big picture.

Be sure to obtain the reports directly from the bureaus, not from a bank. This is because the ones from the bank are written for the lenders. They will not have all of the information that you, who the report is about, will need. A lender's copy from the bank will instead show you information that you will not need like the creditor's member numbers while leaving out things like a list of every company that has bought and seen the report which is useful to you.

Once you have your reports, you will notice that they have four sections. These are identifying information, credit history, public records and inquiries. The first, identifying information, is the information that is used to connect you to the information in the rest of the report. It is what you send in to the bureaus when you are applying for something requiring a credit report and allows them to find it for you. You should make sure the information in this section is accurate but do not be worried if there are variations such as multiple spellings. These stay on the report as they were reported to the bureau that way and are necessary for the information to stay connected.

The next section will be your credit history. Sometimes, you will see "trade lines" listed in this section. Those are the individual accounts in your history. They will all list the name and account number of the creditor. This number may be scrambled as a security measure for the creditor. Sometimes, you will see more than one line or account for a single creditor which is fine. Moving or transferring accounts is common.

Each entry in your credit history will include the following information about it:

- Which kind of credit it was (examples could be revolving credit lines like cards verses mortgage or car loans).
- If this is only a line of credit to you or if it is shared with someone else. Large items like a mortgage or business loan are often shared with a spouse, family member, friend, or business partner.
- The total amount of the credit or the credit limit.
- How much is still owed out of that limit?
- How much the monthly payments are.
- If the account is open, inactive, paid off, or closed.
- How reliably you have paid on the credit account.

In addition to this information, your recent payment history is also included. This will show if you have paid the agreed amount each month and the amount of the payments. This section will show if you have closed an account, it went to collections, if it is charged off or if it is in default. A charge off means that the creditor has given up on getting you to pay your debt. This is not a good thing to have on your credit report.

For each entry on your credit history section, the contact information for each line of credit will also be shown. Take note of this information as it will be useful if you ever have disputes or problems with your creditor.

The third section is public records. These include only the financial data of your records which includes tax liens, judgements, wage garnishment, and bankruptcies. Things like if you have been arrested or had a lawsuit brought against you will not be in your credit report. This really is not a good section to have information in since it always shows that you have had a problem with your finances.

The fourth section is inquiries. This section simply outlines a list of anyone who has asked to see your credit history. This can be a rather long list since as you read above, a lot of people have access to your credit report. It is a very good idea to look at the list of inquiries on your credit report.

You will notice that there are two types of inquiries: hard inquiries and soft inquiries. Hard inquiries are when you are applying for credit and can remain on your report for up for two years and may affect your score. Soft inquiries come from companies, employers, or current creditors. Soft inquiries do not affect your score but also stay on the report for up to two years.

Hard inquiries are the reason it is recommended not to apply for credit very often. If you have too many hard inquiries in a short time frame, it can look like you are in a financial crisis and in need of money. Each one dings your score a little and shows that you might not be able to pay a regular payment. Each hit adds up and eventually, you will not be eligible for credit from most creditors.

Other sections you may find but??? are consumer reports, which are short and voluntary explanations for something in your report. Also included is a separate list of all accounts that are in collections, a list of any disputes you have made and if they have been corrected, with an abridged version of individual entitlements as stated by the act and law of your state law. The sections can be used to your benefit. Be sure to keep the copy of your rights on file for easy access.

Things that are not on your credit report and are not collected by the credit bureaus are a record of bounced checks, your race or ethnicity, sex or gender, income, or political views.

Some information is kept by the credit bureaus but is not going to show up on your credit report such as any negative hits to your report that is no longer going to show up since they are older than the required time. This includes things such as judgements older than seven years, bankruptcies older than ten years, or hard inquiries over two years old.

Sample Credit Report Information

Here are the types of detail one may discover in the report. Check this detail in each of the reports to determine which actions you should take, whether that is paying accounts, contacting creditors, or sending a dispute letter. Also, make sure that everything is accurate. The information in your report will be a good indicator of if your identity has been stolen.

Personal Information:
- Name
- Other Names
- Social Security Number
- Date of Birth
- Telephone Numbers
- Report Date
- Previous Addresses
- Current Address
- Other Identification
- Alert Contact Information
- Previous Employment
- Employers Names
- Employment Locations
- Employment Positions
- Dates Employment was Reported
- Date You Were Hired

Public Records Such as Civil Judgements
- Court Types
- Dates Files
- Date Paid
- Assets
- Responsibility
- Plaintiff
- Attorney
- Amount
- Contact Information
- Estimated Date it will be Removed

Adverse Accounts such as Collections
- Balance
- Pay Status
- Date Verified
- Original Balance
- Original Creditor
- Credit Limit
- Past Due
- Terms for Payment
- Account Type
- Responsibility
- Dates Opened and Closed
- Date Paid
- Creditor Contact Information
- Remarks
- Estimated Date it will be Removed

All Accounts that are in Good Standing
- Balance
- Date Updated
- High Balance
- Collateral

- Credit Limit
- Past Due
- Terms
- Pay Status
- Account Type
- Responsibility
- Date Opened
- Date Closed
- Date Paid
- Loan Type
- Remarks
- Creditor Contact Information
- Estimated Date it will be Removed

Revolving Accounts

- Account Number
- Account Owner
- Type of Account
- Date Opened
- Payment Agreement
- High Credit (highest amount you have used)
- Credit Limit
- Balance
- 3 or More Year Payment History
- Account History (such as raised limits over time)
- Creditor Contact Information

Credit Inquiries:

- Date Requested
- Inquiry Type
- Permissible Purpose (reason for inquiry)
- Contact Information of the Inquirer

Chapter 3

How to Understand and Monitor Your Credit Score

It may be surprising, but your credit score is completely separate from your credit report. You have to order them separately even though your score is determined by relying on the details in the report.

This chapter will explain how your credit score is calculated and how to obtain and monitor your credit score online.

Types of Credit Scores

The most used method of formulating a credit score in the United States is the FICO (Fair Isaac Corporation) scoring system. It is a weighted system in which each section of your credit report has a weight out of 100%. Each negative and positive aspect in your credit report equates to points for its section that either increases or decreases your score. More about the FICO scoring system can be found in this chapter.

FICO also released a new type of scoring system called the NextGen score. They claimed it could increase how many people could qualify for credit. Even though they put a lot of time and money into developing the new scoring system, lenders did not adopt it and now it is rarely if ever used. Individuals can also not access this score.

111

Another type of credit scoring system is the VantageScore. This scoring system was created by the three major credit bureaus in 2006 and competes with the FICO system. It is managed by an independent company called VantageScore Solutions, LLC. VantageScore has some similarities to the FICO system but differs in their analytical method. The two scores cannot be compared.

The FICO Scoring System

In the United States, the FICO (Fair Isaac Corporation) system is used to calculate your credit score. The Fair Isaac Corporation is a company that is based in California and was founded in 1956. It created the FICO score which measures consumer credit risk. This system has become a staple of credit and lending in the United States and is used in a handful of other countries as well.

The FICO scoring system can be explained as a weighted system. Each section of your credit report will have a weight out of 100% that it is worth. Also, each part within a section will contribute to adding or subtracting points.

Any debt you may have contributes to 30% of your FICO score. There are three types of debt that can be included in this section which are revolving debt, instalment debt, and open debt. Revolving debt includes all of your credit cards, retail credit cards, and sometimes a section of a mortgage as defined in your contract. The key thing to pay attention to with revolving debt is the percentage of debt to credit limit. This is often called "open to buy" and "debt-to-credit ratio" on credit reports. This is determined by using the limits to divide the card balance and finding the product with multiplying that by one hundred and is done for your total debt. The higher your percentage in this section is, the lower your credit score will be.

Due to this percentage, it is often a good idea to keep paid off credit cards open, even if you do not plan on using them again. This lowers the percentage of debt to credit and will thus improve your score. For example, if a person has three credit cards which are almost maxed out at a 90% ratio, but they pay one off, their percentage could drop to 75%. However, if they were to close that account, their debt to credit ratio could again increase to 90%. The ratio is what matters to your credit score, and not the direct amount of debt. So, someone who is only a few hundred dollars in debt but has a 100% debt to credit ratio will have a lower score than someone a million dollars in debt with a 50% ratio. This might not seem fair but it is helpful to keep in mind.

The second type of debt in the debt section of your FICO score is called installment debt. Installment debt is a debt where you are paying a fixed payment for a fixed amount of time. This includes things like auto and student loans. Although this type of debt is considered in your score, it does not hold as much importance as revolving type debt. At the same time, it holds more importance to you since it is usually an item such as a car or boat that can be repossessed if not paid.

The third type of debt is called open debt and it is not very common. Open debt means that any balance you accrue must be paid in full each month. The most common of these types of debt is a charge card such as the American Express Green card. This type of debt is considered part of the revolving debt section during calculation of your credit score.

Your payment history is the next part of your FICO score and is worth 35% of your total score. This section is a bit more straight-forward than your debt. It is calculated by looking at any negatives on your record such as collections, repossessions, settlements, liens, charge offs, foreclosures, judgements, late payments, and bankruptcies. Each of these has a different weight based on severity, age, and prevalence. The more you have and the longer they have gone unpaid, the worse off your score will be.

Another section is account diversity. This section of your FICO score only accounts for 10% but should still not be ignored. You will benefit from having a diverse history that includes several types of accounts. It is a good idea to have more than one type of credit history. Aim to have at least two of the possible types of accounts on your record such as a credit card and an auto loan or student loan and a mortgage. All this is proving is that you are capable of managing more than one type of account, but it is still a positive.

How old your credit history is which is also called time in file or credit file age, will also contribute to your FICO score. This is worth 15% of your total score. Your credit age is pretty simple, the older your history the better the score for this section. The age is determined by looking at both the age of your file and the average age of all of your accounts within the file. What they are looking for here is stability. Are you capable of holding an open line of credit for an extended period of time or not? The amount of time since you have last used an open account is also sometimes considered. This is another reason why it is not a good idea to close credit cards even if you no longer want to use them. In fact, it is often recommended to pay bills with a credit card you do not want to use, then immediately pay it off to maintain a good record with the company.

The final section of your FICO score is inquiries and is worth 10% of your score. As explained in the previous chapter, only hard inquiries count against this score. These include inquiries made by lenders when you want to open a new line of credit or loan. It can, but do not always count against your score.

Soft inquiries that do not affect your score include: account management in which an existing creditor checks your files, consumer disclosure which is checking your own credit report, inquiries related to insurance, pre-screening inquiries in which a credit bureau sells some of your information to another institution for marketing purposes, inquiries for employment screening, inquiries related to utilities, and if you give a credit counseling agency permission to view your file.

The importance of each of these categories usually follows the model outlined above. However, those with minimal history might not have information in some of the categories. This means that if you are new to credit, probably because you are a young adult, the weights and relative importance of the categories you do have information in will be different. This also means that if you have a very broad and old credit history, each individual thing will hold less and less importance to the overall score the more you have.

For example, a recent college graduate with student loans as their only source of credit history will have those loans account for almost 100% of their credit score whereas, their parents who have in their lifetime had student loans of their own, two credit cards, a mortgage, paid several utilities, have bought three cars, and are paying on a boat will have much less importance placed on each of these events. This also means that if the same recent graduate got a credit card but allowed it to go into default, the hit to their credit would be much larger than if their parents did the same thing.

It is also important to note that your FICO score only looks at things on your credit report. Things like income and job history do not factor into the score. This is especially useful if you have had trouble finding or holding a job or do not have income for a period of time due to illness. Those life events will not alter your score as long as you still pay on or otherwise form an agreement for your debts with your creditor.

If you obtain your score from a credit bureau, usually through paying, they will often also tell you what the greatest factors that are influencing your score are. You may notice that these are negatives since that is what will lower your score. It is doubtful that something is good enough to make the list for improving your score.

The minimum required data to calculate a FICO credit score is different for each credit bureau but is generally considered to be at least one credit account that is older than six months. It also has to be reported to the credit bureau for over six months. Another requirement that is usually not relevant is that you cannot have a record of deceased on the report. Of course, if you are looking at your credit report it probably means you are not dead yet. However, if you happen to share an account with another person such as your spouse, and they have passed away, this could mean that your score cannot be calculated until you contact your creditor and the credit bureau.

Your score will also be different depending on which credit bureau is used for the score. Just as was explained in the previous chapter, each report is different based on the information they acquire about you. That means that the scores built on these reports will reflect what is found in the reports and thus be slightly different. The information they have will likely still be similar enough that your score will not vary greatly unless you do not have much history. If you have a little credit history, the scores from one bureau might be much higher or lower. Otherwise, you might not meet the minimum requirements to calculate a score at one or more bureaus due to the fact that something has not been reported to all three.

Keep in mind these tips about your credit score:

- You should acquire all of your FICO scores from the three major credit bureaus at the same time as they tend to fluctuate often.
- Not all of your credit information will be updated at the same time since creditors tend to report to the bureaus at different times. This can cause your score to fluctuate month to month and each bureau to have more updated information at different points throughout the month or year.
- Not every score you encounter will be a FICO score. It is imperative to make sure that the scores you are looking at are indeed FICO since that is what most of the creditors will be looking at.
- Each credit bureau will display the information in your report differently, even if it is the same information, which could lead to slight differences in scores.
- Not all of the credit bureaus will have all of your information because creditors choose who they report to.

Lastly, some final information that you should know about your credit score is about how joint accounts and marriage can affect your score. Joint accounts are for situations where one person cannot qualify for a loan alone and so the addition of guarantors, joint account holders, or cosigners is required. This system is often used to help people build or repair credit. However, all people listed on the account are responsible for the payments. This means that if someone missed a payment, it will harm everyone else on the accounts credit score as well.

As for marriage, if you get married you actually will not share a credit score with your spouse. The only things that will affect both people in the marriage are if they have joint accounts together such as a mortgage. This can be used to a couple's advantage if one person's score is better than the other's as they can have joint accounts in which the person with the lower score can build their credit with higher loans and lower interest rates than before the marriage. Care should be taken however since as mentioned above, you cannot access your credit score if someone you hold an account with passes away until you clear their name from the account.

What is a Good Credit Score?

For the FICO scoring system, the scores range from 300 to 850. This generally means that a score of 670 is a good credit score and 800 is considered to be an exceptional score. Below is a list of FICO score ranges, their common rating, an estimate of how many people have a score in each range, and the impact a score in each range will have on an individual.

Credit Score	Rating	Percent of People	Impact
300-579	Poor	17%	You might have to pay a deposit or fee to gain credit, if you are approved at all.
580-669	Fair	20%	You will be considered for some credit opportunities but are not considered a prime borrower.
670-739	Good	22%	You will be considered for most credit opportunities and are unlikely to allow your accounts to become delinquent.
740-799	Very Good	18%	You will be considered for almost all credit opportunities and will likely receive better interest rates.
800-850	Exceptional	20%	You are on the top list for the best interest rates from lenders.

So why does having a good score matter? Your credit score is above all else, a measure of how likely you are to repay what you borrow and if you will repay it on time. They allow anyone who wants to lend you money to decide if you are worth the risk of lending money and how much they can reasonably give you and expect to get back.

All that risk means is that a better score means you will qualify for more loans and at a better interest rate than those who have lower scores. Simply, it means that you could save hundreds to thousands of dollars over time, rent or buy better housing accommodations, be able to buy a new car, get approved for credit cards, and get better deals on services like telephone or internet if your credit score is better.

There are also instances where there are minimum credit scores that are accepted. Some mortgage lenders like the FHA (Federal Housing Administration) require a credit score of a minimum 580 with at least 3.5% down payment. If your score is lower, you will have to pay at least a 10% down payment and meet a host of other requirements. That could mean the difference between owning a house or not and the value of the property you are able to acquire. For example, even for a 100 thousand dollar house, a 3.5% down payment would be $3,500 whereas a 10% down payment would be $10,000. The difference in money you would be required to save prior to buying a home is quite a lot for most people.

How Credit Scoring Can Help You

It might seem like credit is more of a burden than it is worth. There are however some noticeable effects that having a credit score has on the general population. Due to the fact that about 90% of lenders in the United States now use credit scores, primarily FICO scores to determine eligibility for credit, there have been a lot of improvements to the process of gaining and using credit.

One way that credit scores can help people is that you can get loans faster. Now that credit scores are so easily accessible to creditors through the use of online services, getting approved or denied is almost instantaneous. Many credit decisions are settled in minutes to hours, even for large purchases like a mortgage. The process used to take weeks to get an applicant's score and determine if it was above the companies' cutoff point. Smaller credit decisions online or in stores are decided almost right away now.

In the past, there existed rules which could automatically deny you credit for a past mistake on your credit report. Now that the scoring system described above is in place, your past mistakes fade as time goes by. This means that anything you might mess up will not follow you forever and are not dire for your future.

Making the process of gaining credit approval faster means that more credit is available to consumers like yourself. If a creditor is using a credit scoring system to decide eligibility, they can approve more loans in a shorter period of time. This also means that even if you cannot get approved at one lending company, another might have different policies under which your score will be accepted.

Credit rates also tend to be lower with the credit scoring system than before. It was widely adopted due to the increased confidence that lenders have in the people they are establishing loans with. The increased efficiency and confidence also helps to save lending companies money and allows them to offer lower interest rates.

Using a credit scoring system creates a fairer decision making environment as well. With the implementation of a credit score being the primary factor in the acceptance or denial of credit, there is less room for a lender to use their own personal feelings and beliefs to alter the results. Things like race and ethnicity, how old you are, nation of origin, sex or gender, religious beliefs, where you live, or marital status are not included in your credit report or score and thus cannot be used against you as easily.

How to Monitor Your Credit Online

There are a host of websites dedicated to offering you credit reports and scores as well as information on them online. The best websites to access are those connected to the legitimate credit bureaus or the federal government. Be careful with websites that offer soft scores. Obtain your true scores whenever possible. Below is a list of websites to help you gain access to and monitor your credit. The three major credit bureaus will give you access to your report once a year free but you must pay for your score. The other websites offer you slightly less accurate but free scores and are still safe to use.

- Offers you access to all of your three major reports in one location: https://www.annualcreditreport.com/
- Experian, a major credit bureau: https://www.experian.com/
- TransUnion, a major credit bureau: https://www.transunion.com/
- Equifax, a major credit bureau: https://www.equifax.com/personal/
- Offers you free scores and aid in resolving fraud and disputing errors: https://www.truecredit.com/
- Offers you free scores, several resources, and information on types of credit: https://www.creditkarma.com/

Chapter 4

Your Rights

Some of the most valuable knowledge to have as a consumer navigating your credit is what your rights are under the Fair Credit Reporting Act, what your state rights are, and how to use the federal question jurisdiction in your favor. This information will be useful for any questions, concerns, or problems you might have with your credit report.

Your Rights Under the Fair Credit Reporting Act

The Fair Credit Reporting Act, 15 U.S.C. § 1681 (FCRA) is a United States Federal Government Legislation that was originally passed in 1970. This means that the FCRA is applicable in every state. It was enacted to promote the fairness, accuracy, and privacy of consumer information compiled and used by credit bureaus. In order to protect consumers from inaccurate records due to negligent or willful processes, the FCRA regulates how credit reporting agencies and data furnishers collect and distribute personal consumer information. It also regulates specialty agencies such as those that sell information about medical histories, rental histories, and check writing histories. The FCRA is enforced in several ways: through the Consumer Financial Protection Bureau and the US Federal Trade Commission as well as by private litigants.

The FCRA protects you in several ways. Below is an explanation of your rights under the act.

File disclosure is your first right. This is the right to know what is in your files from any consumer reporting agency. As long as you can provide the required identification, you can gain access to your files. In many cases this will be free, such as: if you are a victim of identity theft, unfavorable decision was taken because of the details in your files, fraud has caused inaccurate information to be reported, you are unemployed but are applying for employment within 60 days, or if you are on public assistance. You can also gain access to one disclosure annually from the agencies.

You also have a right to know your credit score. This usually costs you something unlike applying for your report, however, some mortgage lenders will provide you with your score during the transaction with no extra charge.

If the information in your files has been used against you, you have the right to know. Any time the information in any of your consumer reports, not just your credit report, has been used to deny your application for employment, credit, or insurance or has been used to take some other negative action against you, you must be notified. This notification has to include the contact information of the agency that gave the information that led to the decision.

This is why when you are denied credit, you will receive a letter telling you this information. This right is for your protection against false information being used against you because you now have the ability to obtain the same information that was used for the decision. If something is false, you can take action.

You have the right to dispute information that is incomplete or incorrect on your reports. In order to do this correctly, you must be able to identify and provide proof of the error. Then the agency holding that information must investigate it unless the dispute is deemed frivolous.

If the information is proved incomplete, incorrect, or they cannot verify that it is complete and correct, the agency must delete or correct the information. This usually must be completed within 30 days. Agencies also must remove any information that is outdated. To achieve these requirements, agencies must have procedures in place to ensure accuracy whenever possible.

You also have the right to limit pre-screening of your files for credit and insurance offers. What happens is that parts of your information can be sold to credit and insurance companies who want to offer you a service. Then, they can send you unsolicited offers for business. You have the right to stop these offers which will be explained later in this book and any offers you do receive will include a toll-free phone number for you to use to remove your information from their database.

If any of the above rights have been infringed, you have the right to seek damages from any violators and may be able to sue in either state or federal court. Take note that you might have more rights under your state laws than the federal laws. So, it might be more productive to file through the state court system. If it is proven that your FCRA rights have been violated you can recover attorney fees, court costs, actual or statutory damages, and sometimes punitive damages. Punitive damages apply if the violation against you is proven to be willful and are a major deterrent to false reporting. In order to seek damages in court, you must file the suit before either: five years after the violation against you occurred or two years after discovering the violation, whichever is earlier.

Besides your rights, the FCRA also protects you by managing how your information is reported. Lenders must investigate consumer disputes and correct, delete, or verify the information disputed within 30 days, provide accurate and complete information to credit bureaus, and inform consumers when negative information is placed in their records within one month. Such notice can be included on your monthly statements. So, be sure to pay attention to them.

The FCRA also manages who has access to your files from any agency and why. Only those with an actual reason can gain access. Those who are usually able to see the information on your files are a landlord, insurer, creditor, or employer but there are a few other exceptions as already touched on in this book. The people or businesses that do gain access to your information then must follow several regulations in order to not infringe on your rights.

If an employer or possible employer seeks to gain access to your information, they must gain your written consent. Also, they must tell you why they want the information, how they will use it, not misuse it, give you a copy, and allow you time to dispute the information if necessary.

The one exception to this rule is in the trucking industry. When applying to a trucking position, the FCRA has given an employer the exemption of obtaining written permission for consent and allows them to obtain it through oral or electronic means. This is the only change to the law and is reportedly due to truck driver's lack of access to in-person interviews and fax machines while working.

Your State Rights

Each state has its own laws regarding your credit and information security. However, these laws are considered a nullity if the FCRA is in conflict with them. This is because federal laws always take precedence over state laws. This does mean however that if a state law is not in conflict with the FCRA, it stands. This often leads to some states having more protection for the consumers living in them than other states.

Be careful when looking up your state laws. Due to conditions found in FCRA 15 USC 1681t(b)(1)(E) & (F), many state laws created since September of 1996 are not valid. Below you will find a brief summery of state laws regarding the FCRA that are in effect when this book was written, organized alphabetically by state. Any state that does not have applicable laws besides the FCRA or does not have laws that will significantly alter your rights will be omitted from the list for brevity. Be sure to consult a law professional for more information.

Alaska: The have the Alaska Personal Information Act (AS 45.48) which requires a notice be given when personal security has been breached, allows you or an agency to place a security freeze on your credit report, gives additional restrictions regarding use and disposal of your information, allows fraud victims to petition the court for determination of factual innocence, and allows credit card information to be truncated.

Arkansas: They have Arkansas Code 23-67-405 which covers the use of credit information for insurance purposes. It provides that in the state of Arkansas, insurance companies cannot use a credit score for determining eligibility that uses an address or zip code, gender, marital status, income, religion, ethnic group, or nationality and that they cannot deny, cancel, renew, change or base rates on credit information.

Colorado: Their CRS 12-14-3-105.3(1)e covers credit reporting agencies and employment, providing that they cannot report an arrest or conviction past 7 years unless the job will pay more than of $75,000. They also have the Employment Opportunity Act (8-2-126) which states that an employer or prospective employer cannot use credit information for employment purposes unless it happens to be "substantially related" to the position or either the employer or the person being evaluated is exempt from the law. However, this law does not apply to law enforcement agencies, domestic servants and farm laborers, banks and financial institutions, and any employers who have fewer than 4 employees.

Connecticut: Connecticut Public Act 11-23 prohibits employers from using credit when making employment decisions. The only exception is when seeking employment at a financial institution in a position where creditworthiness is related. Connecticut law Section 36a-696 also protects consumers who have been or who will be denied credit based on their credit report by requiring the disclosure of the decision and all information used in the decision within five business days.

Florida: Section 626.9741 states that an insurer must inform both applicants and insured that their credit report or score is being requested and if they make an adverse decision based on that information you must be furnished with a copy of the report and a notification that explains their reason to the applicant or insured person. The insurer also cannot request a credit report or score because of someone's race or other details.

Georgia: the Georgia Fair Business Practices Act (Part 2 of Article 15 of Chapter 1 of Title 10) provides some protections for consumers regarding public records that could have an adverse effect on their ability to obtain employment and the use of this information by consumer reporting agencies such as credit bureaus. The consumer, in this case, must be notified if the information is reported to a consumer report and their information must be secured with strict procedures.

Illinois: The Employee Credit Privacy Act (820 ILCS 70/5) prohibits employers from obtaining an employee or potential employee's credit information and prohibits basing employment decisions on credit information. This does not apply to law enforcement agencies, financial institutions, a debt collector, or a surety business. They also have Deceptive Business Practices Act 815 ILCS 505/2S which provides that no adverse information regarding a cosigner can be reported to a consumer reporting agency without first notifying that person.

Iowa: Credit Information – Personal Insurance laws (515.103) states that an insurer cannot use a credit report or score that uses someone's race, age, gender, marital status, religion, income, national origin, or address and that an insurer cannot deny, cancel, change or base rates, or refuse to renew a personal insurance policy based only on credit information.

Kansas: Chapter 50, Article 7 (KS 50-704) states that credit institutions cannot report an arrest or conviction past 7 years unless the job will pay more than of $75,000.

Maryland: Code of Maryland (COMAR) §14-203(5) states that credit institutions cannot report an arrest or conviction past 7 years unless the job will pay more than of $20,000. Maryland also has more protections in place for consumers against unscrupulous credit repair companies.

Massachusetts: MGL Ch. 93 §52 states that credit institutions cannot report an arrest or conviction past 7 years unless the job will pay more than of $20,000.

Michigan: Credit Services Organizations Act, MCL 445.1822 protects consumers' unscrupulous credit repair companies.

Minnesota: Minnesota Statutes 2003 13C.02 requires disclosure to a consumer in writing in an employer plans to use their credit report and that they must also receive a copy of the report. Minnesota also has a statute that protects consumers from unscrupulous credit repair companies.

Missouri: Missouri protects consumers' unscrupulous credit repair companies.

Montana: Montana Code Annotated 2003 §31-3-112 prevents the reporting of arrests or convictions past 7 on consumer reports and that a consumer must be notified of reports containing a public record that could result in a negative effect on the consumer.

Nevada: Nevada Revised Statutes 598C.150(2) states that reporting agencies cannot disclose adverse information past 7 years and must periodically remove the outdated information from their records. They also have a statute that prevents people from getting a consumer report with the intent to sell the information without disclosing that to the agency.

New Hampshire: RSA 359-B:5 prevents consumer reporting agencies from reporting adverse information past 7 years unless the job will pay more than of $20,000.

New Jersey: the New Jersey Fair Credit Reporting Act C:56.11-28 adds guidelines for what information must be disclosed to a consumer when they request their credit file, how disputed information is handled, and what damages and fees are to be for negligent violations to the FCRA.

New Mexico: They have a statute that states that reporting agencies cannot disclose adverse information past 7 years from the date of release or parole and if it did not result in a conviction or has been pardoned.

New York: New York Consolidated Laws, Article 25, Section 380-j states that that reporting agencies cannot disclose adverse information past 7 years from the date of conviction, release, or parole unless the job will pay more than of $25,000.

North Carolina: Article 2A, §75-60, et seq. sets guidelines for businesses to protect consumer's information.

Oklahoma: Oklahoma House Bill 2492 provides that before an employer requests a credit report that they must provide written notice to the employee or potential employee on how the information will be used and to ask if they want a copy for free.

Oregon: ORS 659A.320 states that an employer or prospective employer cannot use credit information for employment purposes or discriminate in regard to compensation, promotion, conditions, or privileges of employment. However, this law does not apply to law enforcement agencies and financial institutions.

South Carolina: The Consumer Identity Theft Protection Act - §37-20-110 states that a credit reporting agency must notify creditors if the agency knows that an application for new credit has an outdated address for a consumer and that if a credit card issuer receives an application that is different from the one on their file they must call the consumer to verify the change. Additionally, South Carolina allows a consumer that is the victim of identity theft to go to court to obtain proof of their innocence relating to any accounts or crimes in their name.

Washington: Washington's Fair Credit Reporting Act, RCW 19.182 et seq. adds protections for consumers. It gives the permissible purposes that allow a consumer reporting agency to disclose information on a consumer's report to third parties without credit applications. Additionally, RCW 19.182.040 states that consumer reporting agencies cannot disclose adverse information past 7 years unless the job will pay more than of $20,000.

West Virginia: They have a statute that protects co-signers if the account is not paid. The co-signer cannot be held liable unless they receive and sign a separate notice that explains their liability.

Wisconsin: Wisconsin has protections for consumers against unscrupulous credit repair companies.

Federal question jurisdiction

Federal question jurisdiction is the subject-matter jurisdiction to hear a civil case because the plaintiff has claimed there has been a violation of federal law and the United States is a party. That is a lot to unpack if you are unfamiliar with some of the legal terms used in that definition.

To begin, a civil case involves a private dispute between two or more people or organizations. This is not the same as a criminal case in which someone is suspected of committing a crime and is then brought to court because of the offence. A plaintiff is a person that brought the case to court against another person or organization. The other party in a case is called the defendant. They are the one in a civil case that has been either sued or accused by the plaintiff.

What it means for a court to have subject-matter jurisdiction is that the court has the power to decide a case. When federal question jurisdiction applies is if the lawsuit arises under federal law. Federal laws include the United States Constitution, the United States Code (statutes), the United States Code of Federal Regulations, and treaties in which the United States is a party. Any lawsuit based on a federal law should allow the federal court to have subject-matter jurisdiction over the case, making it federal question jurisdiction.

The FCRA is a federal law, therefore if your rights under this law have been infringed upon; your case will fall under federal question jurisdiction. In the case of disputes involving credit, there are two ways the case can fall. One is when you would be the plaintiff and you would be bringing a civil case against a creditor or credit bureau under the FCRA. Other laws that can be violated by a creditor are the Fair Debt Collection Practices Act (FDCPA) and the Telephone Consumer Protection Act (TCPA).

Federal question jurisdiction has no minimum amount requirement for controversy. This means that even if the amount you want to dispute or the damages you are seeking are not very large or if you are not seeking a payment at all, you can still take your case to court to resolve your problem.

Most of the time, you will not gain a lot in damages or fees. Most of the time, your attorney's fees will be covered and you will get $1,000. If you have been harmed due to the violation, you can receive more, however. Another thing to keep in mind when bringing a creditor to court is that you might still be liable to pay the debt, even if you win the case.

The opposite can also be true. The second scenario in a civil case is that you can be sued by a creditor for not paying your debts. In that case, you would be the defendant. However, if this happens to you it is possible to challenge the debt. Make sure that if you are brought to court, you do not pay advance fees to any debt solution company and to get help from an accredited counselor or attorney. Also, be sure to always respond to court summons otherwise you might lose the case by default.

You can challenge your debt by invoking your rights under the FCRA. If your creditor has violated any of your rights explained above or taken any of the actions against you, they may lose the case.

A creditor or debt collector cannot:

- Threaten you or your loved ones with violence
- Use foul language when communicating with you
- Seize any of your belongings unless they have gone through the proper legal routes
- Lie about you owing a debt
- Call at an unreasonable time of day, defined as from 9:00 PM to 8:00 AM
- Call repeatedly in an effort to pressure you into paying your debt
- Call your place of work or anyone besides you, your family, and your attorney about your debt
- Contact you directly when you are already represented by a legal representative
- Claim that you will be arrested for not paying your debt
- Pretend to be anyone besides who they are such as a lawyer or government official.

Chapter 5

How to Remove Negative Records

If you find a problem on your credit report your biggest help will be knowing how to dispute that information. You now know the basics of what laws protect you. This chapter will tell you how to take advantage of your rights and challenge credit bureaus over incorrect and damaging information using simple methods, the most prominent of which will be dispute letters.

You can use dispute letters to remove a lot of negative information from your credit report. However, this chapter will also give you tips besides using dispute letters alone. You will learn how to stop all collections and how to delete late payments, inquiries, charge offs, collections, judgments, and tax liens from your credit report. The following chapter will give you sample letters to use as templates in the process.

Many people face mistakes in their report. It has even been estimated that about one fifth of consumers have found errors in their reports from one of the three major credit bureaus. Less likely but still far too common is when an error on your report causes you to get bad rates on loans or insurance. About one in twenty people have lost money due to mistakes.

Viewing these odds makes it all the more important for you to understand what is in your credit report and how to fix any mistakes. Chances are that it could happen to you or someone you know.

Mistakes could be accounts that are not yours, wrong amounts, or false claims of account delinquency. If anything like this is on your report, you need to file a dispute. Otherwise, it will remain on your record and cause you and your score harm.

You may have noticed that each credit report you receive will come with a web address for the credit bureaus' online dispute forms. <u>These forms are fine to use but are not as effective as sending written correspondence, especially if the error on your report is a major problem. Although you are free to use their online services, the reasons why using a letter is the better method are explained in more detail below.</u>

The FCRA requires credit bureaus to investigate any dispute you make and respond to you within 30 days of the dispute. This time limit is extended to 45 days if you provide more information regarding the dispute during this period. You can see that the item(s) being disputed are under investigation on your credit report as they are marked as disputed until a resolution has been made or the information is proven to be accurate.

If the credit bureaus' decision is not satisfactory to you or you find your case being handled carelessly, you should file a complaint at the company. You can do this online with the Consumer Financial Protection Bureau and with the company in question. You can also request that the fact that you filed a dispute and it was not resolved to your satisfaction be noted on all of your future credit reports. That statement can be sent to those who have seen your report prior to the change.

Being denied insurance, credit, or employment or being given bad credit terms based on the information that is in your credit report is not an ideal situation. So, what can you do about it? First of all, if that happened to you, you should have received a notification from the insurance company, lender, or employer with the contact information of the credit bureau that they used for the information to make the decision.

Within sixty days of receiving this notice, you are legally entitled to a free report from that credit bureau. Make sure you take advantage of this free report and review the information. If there is an error that influenced the decision, you can dispute both the error with the credit bureau and company that provided the credit bureau with the information. If the error has caused damages, you can seek compensation in court as explained in the last chapter.

When your dispute investigation is completed, you will also receive a written notice of the results from where you filed your dispute. If your information was indeed inaccurate, all three of the nationwide credit bureaus will also be notified to correct their information if necessary. You will also be entitled to another free credit report if the dispute results in a change to the information on it. Additionally, if any information is removed or changed, a credit bureau cannot include it in your report again unless it is verified to be correct and complete.

If any information on your report changes, you can request that a copy with the notice of any corrections that were made be sent to any person or company that saw your report within the last six months. For employment, anyone who received your report within two years prior to the change can be sent a copy and notification as well.

Online Correspondence

As mentioned above, you can do most of these steps online. There is information in your credit report on how to file a dispute in this manner and nearly all credit bureaus have information on filing electronically on their websites as well. This method is quick and easy and many consumers think that it will work the same as a physical letter. What they do not tell you is that if you file your complaint online, there are several benefits it grants credit bureaus that can harm you.

One important reason to use a physical copy of a dispute letter is that there is a physical record of your dispute and the date you filed it with the credit bureau. In order to have records of both when you sent the letter and when the company received it, be sure to send any letter to a credit bureau with certified mail which will be explained in chapter eight of this book.

Why it is important to have a date on record of when you filed the dispute is because the bureaus are required to remove all information that they cannot verify within 30-45 days. If there is no record of the date that investigation period starts on, they can take advantage of that and either take longer or fail to comply at all. Often, when you file a dispute online you will not receive proper notification or confirmation of the request either which makes it hard to pinpoint the date for official records.

Another reason that it is not a good idea to file your dispute online is that the FCRA was revised to include online disputes and it was not in your favor. In Section 611a (8) of the FCRA, the credit bureau is allowed to disregard some of the laws in place to protect you if they delete the information you disputed within three days.

Whereas your rights usually include the ability to send a copy of your report and a notice of what was changed to the other bureaus, your creditors, and others who have seen your report, it is not required under this law. They also do not have to send you the results of the dispute investigation in writing or show how they came to their conclusions if you file online. This will make it difficult for you to move forward or complain if you do not like the results.

To make matters worse is that the definition of "delete" in this law can mean that the false information is only temporarily removed from your reports and can be placed in your file again if the creditor reports the wrong information again. This can happen in only about a month after filing your first dispute, requiring you to start the process again.

Removing Late Payments, Charge-offs, and Collections

Late payments, charge-offs, and collections all harm your credit substantially and should be dealt with in some way. There are a few ways to accomplish this but we will focus on using dispute letters as they are effective in the most situations.

Late payments tend to become charge-offs and then go to collections so dealing with your late payments first is a good idea. How you decide to deal with your late payments depends a lot on both your general credit history as well as your history with the company you are late with.

First of all, you should understand how late payments, charge-offs, and collections effect your credit. The longer they are past due is the most important factor, not how much the payment is worth. Taking this into consideration can prevent a majority of your late payments. Say you have three payments due but only enough money to cover either the two smaller or one larger amount. Knowing your credit is affected by the time and number of accounts past due, you should logically pay the two smallest accounts first, preventing at least one late payment.

You should also note that your late payment will not automatically be reported. Depending on the situation, it will take a minimum of 30 days to show up on your credit report and might not show at all until you close the account. Unless you are late by at least 30 days, it will not show up at all. Also know that even if you pay off a late-payment, charge-off, or collection, it will still show up in your credit report unless you do something else about it.

If you are 90 days late, it can be turned into a charge-off but you can still pay if you are that late to try and avoid charge-offs, collections, and even repossessions.

The good news is that you can also remove the record of late payments, charge-offs, and even collections. Some good methods to achieving this that are??? not dispute letters??? are either requesting a goodwill adjustment from your creditor or offering to sign up for automatic payments. A goodwill adjustment is a good option for those with a good history. What you do is send a letter that asks the creditor to forgive a late payment in a way that explains how you have been a good client, what went wrong, and why you would like to have the record removed. A sample goodwill adjustment letter will be explained in the next chapter.

Another option is to sign up for automatic payments. This can work, even if you have been a repeat offender with late payments but will likely only remove your most recent late payment. Why this works is that you are giving the creditor a more concrete commitment to pay on time in the future. You do have to make sure that the money is in your checking account when it is scheduled to be withdrawn so you might find that this is not a good choice for you.

Probably the best way to remove late payments is with a letter which will be explained further below.

As for charge-offs, you should first consider if it would be a better use of your time and money to just pay it off. It will still show up in your report this way but will be less of a blemish than if it is left unpaid. You should pay a charge-off if it is recent if you are trying to qualify for a home loan, if you have an agreement with the creditor for it to be deleted or re-aged if you pay it. You should not pay a charge-off if it is listed for multiple companies, you do not know if you actually owe the amount shown, or if it is past the statute of limitations.

Any negotiations you do with the company that is holding your charge-off can be done over the phone, but like most things involving credit, it is best to do it all in writing to have physical records.

While it might be harder to remove collections from your credit report, it can still be done. Review the rules in the FCRA and in your state for the statutes of limitations and the timeline you have to work with prior to starting the process of removing collections since they are the most sensitive to work with and you could inadvertently harm your credit in the long run. Many people find this too difficult and seek professional help but that is not always necessary. Choose the route that is best for you.

Accounts that remain unpaid for four to six months, depending on the company, get sent to collections. You might not be contacted about your debt during this time. That is a signal that you need to do something about the debt. People often get caught off-guard by nasty collection calls and letters if they do not remember or understand their debt.

Unlike late payments and charge-offs, paying your collections account will not improve your credit score. So, take that into account with your negotiations. Also, make sure that you still owe the collection since debt buyers will buy your debt for less than it was originally worth and the statute of limitations might be over.

Send a validation request to the collection agency that is listed on your credit report to confirm that they own the debt and to start correspondence. They have to send you the proof in writing that they do own your debt and if you still owe it.

Do not pay on debt in collections unless you know what the statute of limitations and the reporting date are. If you pay on an account, it will re-age it, making it stay on your credit report longer than necessary. If you are coerced into paying without knowing this information, it is illegal under the FCRA and you should seek legal counsel. You might even be open to a lawsuit which can lead to a judgement on the account.

If you try these other methods and they do not work or they are not suitable for your situation, you can try sending a dispute letter directly to the credit bureau. You can only do this if some of the information is incorrect or unverifiable. Otherwise, it will not be removed.

Comb through your records to locate any information such as the dates, payment amounts, and any other pertinent information is correct on your credit report. If you find anything, you can file a dispute by sending a dispute letter to all of the credit bureaus that list the incorrect information. If they cannot verify the information it must be removed from your report which if it works in your favor, could have entire negative records removed for you.

How to Remove Judgments

Judgements are one of the worst things that you can have on your credit report and they have lasting consequences. Since they are the result of a court-ordered mandate to repay a debt, they are different that if something goes to collections. Judgments could happen to anyone and can be the result of a wide range of factors including alimony, failure to pay child support, civil and small claims lawsuits, and more. You might not be able to get new credit at all if you have a judgement on your report and if you do get approved, it will be at one of the highest interest rates possible.

Even though judgments are a harsh thing to have, you can have them removed from your credit report before the usual date. Most of the time, a judgement will be on your credit report for seven years from the filing date.

Something to consider when trying to vacate judgements is which type of judgement you have. An unsatisfied judgement is the most damaging and results from an unpaid and unsettled lawsuit. A satisfied judgement is one that has been paid or settled. This is the ideal situation and can be achieved through paying it in full, negotiating a settlement, filing bankruptcy, or having it collected by force which usually involves wage garnishment.

A vacated judgement has been dismissed through an appeal in court. This type will not appear on your credit report and can be disputed through the use of a dispute letter if it does. Making your judgement vacated is the best way to remove it from your record but requires filing a motion in court to appeal the ruling against you.

The last type of judgement is re-filed judgements. These can arise if your judgement has been renewed, leading to it remaining on your credit report for an additional seven years. In some states, this can happen indefinitely for the rest of your life meaning you need to take action to make it satisfied as soon as possible.

To remove a judgement, there are essentially two ways to go about it on your own:

1) Getting the court to validate the judgement in order to ensure that all of the details are correct on your credit report. If the court cannot or will not do this for you, it is often the case that you can simply dispute it with the credit bureaus to have it removed from your credit report.

2) Make sure that any information you get from the court is accurate as if you find anything reported incorrectly, you are able to file a dispute to have it removed.

How to Remove Tax Liens

Tax liens are likely the most serious thing you will find on your credit report and have far reaching consequences. They can lead to tax levies which allow the government to seize your property to satisfy your debts. This can include your bank accounts, retirement accounts, car, personal property such as jewelry and technology, business assets, and home or land.

Even worse is that if it is left unpaid, they can stay on your record forever. A paid tax lien will still remain on your record for seven years and having one makes it impossible to sell your home or qualify for any new credit.

Due to the fact that tax liens are public records, you must work with both the credit agencies and the IRS in order to remove them from your credit report. You will also not be informed if you have a tax lien until it is on your credit report making it impossible to work out beforehand.

If this happens to you, be absolutely sure to keep every record you receive involving the lien. If you find any discrepancies, you can file a dispute to have it removed from your credit report. Often times even if you dispute, since it is likely to be a large debt, it still will not be removed from your record. You also cannot avoid a tax lien through bankruptcy as a bankruptcy will not include your tax liens unless it is filed prior to when the lien is placed on your record.

146

The main way to get a lien off of your record is to pay it off and wait for the seven years period for it to fall off of your record. This is certainly not an ideal situation and thankfully there is a way to remove it from your report if you need to qualify for housing, a car, or other credit.

To remove a lien, you have to request a withdrawal while still making payments using IRS form 12277. You will still have to pay the tax lien completely and pay according to the payment plan. Then you still have to contact both the credit bureaus and the IRS to notify them of the change in your liens status. This is sometimes also possible if it has been paid off already, but you still have to follow the strict guidelines set out by the IRS. Due to the nature of tax liens, a professional will likely be able to guide you through this long and tedious process better than going alone.

Cease and Desist Letters for Debt Collectors

If you have been working on removing negative aspects of your credit but it has become overwhelming, cease and desist letters can help stop the endless stream of calls and letters you are bound to receive. Section 805 (c) of the Fair Debt Collection Practices Act (FDCPA) gives you the right to ask collection agencies to stop contacting you and they must comply.

Cease and desist letters must be written and sent to the debt collection agencies that hold your debt USPS certified mail, for proof of delivery. It's also good to include what you are disputing and alleging in the letter, and give them only 30 days to provide proof of debt, if they do not respond in 30 days they have to remove the negative reporting. A sample letter will be included and explained in the next chapter.

Just because you send a cease and desist letter does not mean that your debt is removed, just that the collection agencies cannot contact you directly in an attempt to get you to pay. Your debt will still show up on your record and the collection agency may try to sue you for the payment.

Sending this kind of letter is a gamble. The collection agency could either pursue a legal action or, less likely, stop pursuing you completely. The outcome will mostly rest on how much the debt is; the larger the amount, the less likely the agency will be to let it go. If it is a small amount or about to reach the statute of limitations, it is more likely that they will decide that it is not worth their time or money to bring it to court. Do not count on them letting it go though, by sending a cease and desist letter you are essentially provoking the collection agency.

Once you send the letter, the agency can contact you only one more time in writing to notify you of the actions they are going to take.

A cease and desist letter should only take you 10 minutes to type up and sign.

Chapter 6:

Correspondence Letter Templates

The previous chapter explained how to remove negative records from your credit report as simply as possible. This chapter will continue with that theme since the removal of negative records can be the quickest and most important way to improve your credit score. This chapter is organized to explain how to write different correspondence letters that will be necessary for your journey and then gives you an example that you can use. There are three types of letters that we will cover here: dispute letters, cease and desist letters, and goodwill letters.

You are free to use these templates as they are, but they should be tailored to your specific situation. It is best if you use them as mere guidelines and write the letter yourself. If you are not confident in your skills in completing this, it might be best to seek help in writing the letters.

Dispute Letters

Dispute letters are the most variable of the three types of written correspondence that will be explained in this book. Their various applications were outlined in the previous chapter. The simple explanation of when to use dispute letters is any time you find information on your credit report that you find questionable, inaccurate, incorrect, or incomplete. Dispute letters are useful for removing or changing information about charge offs, collections, repossessions, tax liens, credit inquiries, judgments, foreclosures, bankruptcies, and more.

It is important to remember that disputing positive items on your credit report is not recommended, even if the information is wrong because it is difficult to get something placed back onto your record once it is removed. Be sure that you truly want something removed from your credit report and know what the effects of doing so will be prior to starting this process.

It is also recommended that you contact the creditor that supplied the information to the credit bureaus before sending a dispute letter to the bureaus. It might be as simple as a phone call to your creditor to resolve an error on your reports.

If you need to file a dispute, ensure that you have all of your supporting information that will be needed. That should include any statements, bills, notices, receipts, phone call records, emails, or other related information. You will also need a hard copy of your credit report or other evidence that the error exists and copies of two forms of identification such as ID, social security card, passport, W-2 form, utility bill, or pay stub. You should mark the error on your credit report or other evidence in an obvious manner such as by circling it. Always make sure to send copies of information and keep the originals for your records.

To write a dispute letter you should:

- Use professional yet kind language that does not reflect anger or hostilities towards the credit bureaus.

- Make sure that any information you include in your letter in supports of your claims cannot be used against you.

- Make your request clear and concise. Have someone you trust proofread the letter for you as well.

- Send your letter via certified mail.

To write a dispute letter, you should not:

- Send original copies of any documents. It is crucial to have originals for your own records.

- Mention any of the laws or procedures. The credit bureaus are already aware of this information.

- State the results of court proceedings or threaten lawsuits against the credit bureaus.

Dispute Letter Template

Date

Your Name

Your Address

Your City, State, Zip Code

Complaint Department

Name of Credit Bureau

Address

City, State, Zip Code

Dear Sir or Madam,

 I am writing to dispute the following information in my credit report. I wish to dispute the item(s) that is/are encircled on the attached copy of the report I received on [date]. This/These item(s), [identify which item you are referring to and its source] is inaccurate/incomplete because [identify what is inaccurate and why]. Please provide evidence that this information is correct and that my rights have not been infringed upon. In the case that no evidence exists, please [delete/correct/change] this account information as soon as possible.

Sincerely,

Your Name

Signature

Account Name

Account Number

Your report or confirmation number (if available)

Enclosures: (List what you are enclosing)

Cease and Desist Letters

The reasons that you might want to send a cease and desist letter and the pros and cons of doing so were explained in the last chapter. You want to include your contact information and the account number that you want to stop being contacted about. Use this as a last resort for stopping collection companies as it can backfire, leading to your case being brought to court. Writing a cease and desist letter is quite different from writing a dispute letter. Pay attention to their differences.

To send a cease and desist letter you should:

- Use professional yet firm language.

- Reference the Fair Debt Collections Practice Act (FDCPA).

- Keep all original copies for your records.

- Send your letter via certified mail.

  To send a cease and desist letter you should not:

- Incriminate yourself in anything that the collection agency might have accused you of doing.

- Use personal language.

Cease and Desist Letter Template

Date

Your Name

Your Address

Your City, State, Zip Code

Name of Collection Agency

Address

City, State, Zip Code

Re: Account Number

To [Name of Collection Agency],

Under the provisions of the Fair Debt Collections Practices Act (FDCPA), Public laws 95 – 109 and 99 – 361, I am formally notifying you to cease all communications with me regarding my debt for this account and any other debts that you have purported that I owe.

I will file a complaint with the Federal Trade Commission and the [Your State] Attorney General's office as well as pursue criminal and civil claims against you and your company if you attempt to continue contacting me after you receive this notice. If I receive any further communications after you have confirmed receipt of this notice, the communications may be recorded as evidence for my claims against you.

You should also be aware that any negative information related to this account on my credit reports will be handled with all legal rights available to me.

Regards,

Your Name

Signature

Goodwill Letters

Goodwill letters were also explained in the previous chapter. They are not a guaranteed method of removing negative information from your credit report but are still worth a try in some situations. They are more effective if you have a good history with the company, have had a technical error delayed your payment, or if your autopay did not go through. You can sometimes even convince a credit company to forgive a late payment if you simply forgot to pay.

Try to contact your credit agency by phone to negotiate and explain your situation before sending a goodwill letter. This tactic might be all that you need to do in order to remove the record of the late payment. The sooner you contact, the better as well. If you notice that you have a late payment, calling right away could stop it from being reported at all.

To write a goodwill letter you should:

- Use courteous language that reflects your remorse for the late payment and thank the company for their service.
- Include reasons you need to have the record removed such as qualifying for a home or auto loan or insurance.
- Accept that you were at fault for the late payment.
- Explain what caused the payment to be made late. To write a goodwill letter you should not:
- Be forceful, rude, or flippant about the situation.

Goodwill Letter Template

Date

Your Name

Your Address

Your City, State, Zip Code

Name of Credit Company

Address

City, State, Zip Code

Re: Account Number

Dear Sir or Madame,

Thank you [company's name] for continued service. I am writing in regard to an urgent request concerning a tradeline on my credit reports that I would like to have reconsidered. I have taken pride in making my payments on time and in full since I received [name of credit line/card] on [date that you received the credit]. Unfortunately, I was unable to pay on time [date of missed payment(s)] due to [detailed and personal reason for not being able to pay on time. You might want to include several sentences using as much information as possible to plead your case.]

[Follow up your reason for not paying on time with a concession of guilt such as:] I have come to see that despite [reason listed above], I should have been better prepared/more responsible with my finances to ensure the payment was on time. I have worked on [some type of learning or way of improving your situation] in order to prevent this situation from happening again.

I am in need of/about to apply for [new credit line such as a home loan] and it has come to my attention that the notation on my credit report of [credit company's] late payment may prevent me from qualifying or receiving the best interest rates. Due to the fact that this notation is not a reflection of my status with [credit company], I am requesting that you please give me another chance at a positive credit rating by revising my tradelines.

If you need any additional documentation or information from me in order to reach a positive outcome, please feel free to contact me.

Thank you again for your time,

Sincerely yours,

Your Name

Signature

Chapter 7

Preventing Fraud

Fraud is a terrible thing that can happen to anyone. If your information is stolen, it can be used against you. The person who stole even a little of your information will be able to open accounts in your name for their own use. If you don't do anything about them, you will be liable to pay off that person's debt! Thankfully, there are a lot of things that you can do both to prevent your information from being stolen in the first place and that you can do to repair the damage if it happens to you. This chapter will explain how your information is stored and secured, what kind of companies have your financial and personal data, what the security risks are and how they relate to identity theft, and techniques to lock down your credit report.

How is Consumer Information Stored, Secured, and Used?

To begin, you should know a bit about how your information is stored, secured, and used. If you have a bank account, credit card, phone plan, internet, television, utilities, online banking service such as PayPal, a mortgage, a car loan, of social media such as Facebook or Twitter, your personal and financial information will be stored on servers owned by those companies. These types of services typically have strict guidelines about who can see your information and for what purposes.

The information security of a company should be preventing unauthorized access to your information by utilizing a risk management program that uses standards for passwords, encryption software, antivirus and firewall software, training standards and a legal liability policy.

This does not mean that all of these standards are regularly met and upkept, cannot be broken by outside influence, or cannot be outright circumvented due to provisions in a company's privacy policy that you are required to accept when accessing their web content. It is easy for outside companies and individuals to acquire, analyze, and transfer your information. Companies that do this are called information or data brokers and will be covered more below.

Relating information security to your credit while taking the above information into consideration, you can see how easy it can be for people to use your information against you using the system designed to secure it. If a person is able to obtain information regarding your credit such as a previously owned credit card, they can use that information to open a new line of credit under your name while simultaneously taking advantage of privacy laws which make it difficult to expose them.

For example, if you have a credit card and throw away a bill or statement or have a weak password on your online account, someone could find out your name, payment history, credit limit, the age of the account, phone number, address, and maybe even your social security number. This information will give them enough to steal your identity and open a new line of credit that they are not responsible for.

Then, due to privacy policies and laws, unless you are able to prove ownership of the account to the credit company, you will not be able to obtain information about it or close it without the use of legal intervention. The perpetrator that stole your information is meanwhile able to rack up hundreds to thousands of dollars in purchases while you are working through the process of closing the account. Normally, it is a good thing that people cannot access other people's accounts without having proof of ownership, but it will work against you if your identity is stolen.

It is also staggeringly easy for information from most major companies including data brokers, to be hacked. Even, Equifax which you have heard a lot about in this book and is otherwise a fairly reputable credit reporting agency was hacked in April and September of 2017.

Data Brokers

Typically, it is impossible to find out which data brokers hold your information, how they acquired it, how they use it, who they sell it to, or how long they hold on to it. They usually compile information from thousands of people into the list such as rich people, parents, or doctors. Sometimes more detailed lists are produced such as seniors with dementia, police officers, financially vulnerable people, and more. It has been estimated that about 3500 data broker companies exist, and there could be upwards of 4000 or more.

In the United States, some of the most well-known data brokers including Experian, CoreLogic, Inome, Recorded Future, Acxiom, Cambridge Analytica, Epsilon, Datalogix, and PeekYou. These companies claim to hold millions of people's information and create psychological profiles on them for use mainly in marketing.

They collect your information from other companies, public records, and most often in recent times, your internet history. Every time you browse social media, shop online, search online or use a website, your actions are likely to be tracked and analyzed. This practice results in things like internet advertisements and junk email that is targeted towards your interests, thoughts, and habits.

Common practices of data brokers besides compiling your information are selling products in order to identify financially vulnerable consumers and providing information about consumer offline behavior for use in marketing. The information is then used in dubious practices like discrimination in opportunities services and pricing. A good example of this would be from a White House report in May of 2014 that discovered people with black-seeming first names like Jermaine were more likely than people with white-seeming first names like Geoffrey to be shown ads including the word "arrest."

Identify Theft

After reading this far in this chapter, you probably want to know more about how identity happens and what you can do about it. Identity theft is very common and people can even make a living with it. It happens usually without your knowledge when you do everyday things like browsing online or paying bills using online bank services.

What information are identity thieves looking to steal?
- Name

- Address

- **Birthday**

- Social Security Number

- Driver's License/ID Card Numbers

- Bank Account Numbers

- Credit Card Account Number or Card Information

- Common Security Answers like Your Mother's Maiden Name, Pet's Name, First Job, or School Mascot

If a thief gets even a portion of this short list of information, they are able to open credit cards, open bank accounts, collect various government benefits, shop both offline and online, sign up for phone, internet, and other utilities, pay for adult websites, download music, movies and games, gamble online, rent cars, and even book entire vacations.

So how can people gain this information? One of the easiest and most common techniques is to do what is called "shoulder surfing" which entails looking over your shoulder when you use public computers, your own computer in public, at a sales counter, or at an ATM. When you log into websites, they will be on the lookout for your passwords. Another common and easily accessed method of getting your information is by looking at your social network and dating site profiles. If you have low security settings your name, the city of residence, home town, previous and current employment, pets and family members' names, education, political views, how much money you make, and more can be accessed by strangers without the need for hacking.

People can also access your information by rummaging through your mailbox, garbage, or recycling outside of your home. If you happen to misplace or lose your wallet, purse, laptop, or cell phone or if they are stolen, people have access to a wealth of your information there as well.

Other offenders will use their position to access your information. An example would be someone in an IT department in a company. They can easily gain information about almost any employee or client of that company if they chose to do so. Just as terrible is when someone pretends to be a representative from a reputable company or as a government official in order to send fake emails or texts, call you, or create fake websites in order to trick you into giving them the information you would normally freely give those people.

Online or on public computers, people can deploy spyware which is malicious software designed to steal information about the one who is using the program. They can also just plain hack into computer networks, Wi-Fi networks, and databases. This is usually a tactic used to divert your personal emails to the hacker. They can find out and log into your bank account, social media accounts, and more using this method. Another hacking method is forcing themselves into accounts by guessing or cracking passwords. A less-known online method is to set up a fake job listing in an effort to get people's resumes.

Sometimes people can scan old technology for hidden personal information as well. Old computers, mobile phones, tablets, or portable memory like USB drives can have your information on them. ATMs and point of sale terminals are also notorious for hackers.

There are several ways you can find out that your identity is being used by someone other than yourself. Some things to look for include: being alerted by your bank or credit card about suspicious transactions, being contacted about debt that you did now know about, your bills and statements are late or never arrive, bills arrive for accounts that you did not open, you find purchases or withdrawals on bills or statements that you do not recognize or discovering a tax lien has been placed against you for debt you do not recognize.

If any of these reasons or something else makes you think you have been a victim of identity theft, there are some things you should do right away. Make sure to contact the police and file a report. Keep the number of your report for your records. Call all of your banks and credit card issuers. Their numbers should be on the back of the cards, on your bills and statements, and on their website. Contact the United States Postal Service if your mail is missing. Report the issue to the Federal Trade Commission (FTC). You will also need to contact the three major credit bureaus to place a fraud alert on your credit report. You can do that by phone. Another key thing to complete is IRS Form 14039, Identity Theft Affidavit. You will need to complete this form in writing and mail it in.

Overall, make sure to keep detailed records of every step you take. Write down every phone call with the name of the company, the name of who you speak with, the date and time, and what you reported or requested during the call. Keep copies of everything you send in the mail including originals of statements, bills, and notices. Also, keep the information from the post office for all certified mail you send.

How to Protect Yourself Online

Online methods for stealing or otherwise obtaining your information to use against you are common and diverse. Everyone who uses any type of internet service should educate themselves on how to protect their personal and financial information online. Not allowing your identity to be stolen in the first place is the simplest way to avoid the issue.

Start out by choosing strong passwords. You should never use simple words or the names of your pets, friends, or family. Above all, never choose passwords that can be cracked easily such as "password" or a string of numbers like "12345". Once you have a password, you should never use automatic login features. Not using these can help safeguard your information if your device is stolen or hacked. Just commit to typing your passwords each time you log in. Whenever available, use 2-step verification to log in. This service will ask for your password and then use a secondary method to make sure you are the one accessing the account such as sending a text message to you.

Be careful when sharing your information. Think carefully about what you are sharing about yourself in any networking website or email. Do not post your address, hometown, workplace, or phone number online and avoid posting things about being out of town for long periods of time, especially publicly. If you are ever asked for personal information like the things listed above, ensure that you know why it is needed and what it will be used for prior to submitting the information. The information you should be especially careful about online is your credit card number and social security number. Never put these online without first verifying you are using official and secure websites.

When shopping online, only purchase from companies you can verify and trust. Do not save card information to websites and clear the information in your web browsers cache after banking or shopping online.

If you are using email, only log in using a secure connection. If you are using a website for your email, a message of "secure" or an image of a lock will appear next to the web address if the website is secured. This feature can also be observed on legitimate shopping and social media websites.

Do not reply or click on links in suspicious messages in email or chat services. People often send out spam messages or messages meant to look like they are from someone who wants to contact you. Never open attachments or click on anything in these emails. They can use those to initiate downloads of malware that will collect information from your computer and in some cases destroy it in the process. You should also always have anti-spyware software and an active firewall on your devices.

Another common email scam is posing as service providers like your utilities, a store, or PayPal, a financial institution such as your bank, or a government representative in order to ask you for your personal information. A common method is using an email format from a reputable source and copying it into their own email address with false links. If you enter the fake links provided, it will likely be made to look like the official website. However, when you input your information you will not find your account and the fake website will now have stored your login information to use on the real website.

If this happens to you, immediately log into the real website and change your password.

Use caution when using public Wi-Fi networks. You can usually find public networks in locations like restaurants, libraries, and airports. They are not secure. If you are using a public Wi-Fi network and using passwords or sending private information, it can be stolen by someone else using the network. Do not allow your phone to use Wi-Fi constantly while in public.

As for your personal internet service, you should always have it password protected. Most service providers will set up a new account with a password already in place but it is a simple matter to apply one yourself. Do not use easily guessable or personal information for your password such as your address, name, or phone number. You should also always turn file sharing off on all of your devices. File sharing allows anyone using the same internet network to access your files and often even see what you are doing.

Additionally, make sure to physically secure your devices. Never leave your phone, tablet, or laptop where it can easily be taken or looked at while you are away. At a coffee shop alone and need to use the restroom? It might seem like a pain but always make sure to pack everything up and take it with you rather than ask someone to watch your items. You cannot tell who could try to steal your information. Also, never leave these items in your car, even if it is locked.

If you want to dispose of an item, ensure that it is completely wiped before throwing it away or selling it. Most devices come with a setting that does this however if someone knows what they are doing, can easily restore all of your files if that is the only step you take. Purchase software to hard wipe the drives or even better, take it to a professional to remove the physical drive and destroy it. If you are throwing the device away, have some fun destroying it yourself. Just make sure the memory is thoughohly destroyed as even if the entire device seems destroyed, the memory can still be implanted into another computer.

Credit Freeze

A credit freeze will allow you to restrict access to your credit report. You may have also heard this called a security freeze. The main point of freezing your credit is to prevent identity thieves from opening accounts in your name. It works because credit companies usually have to see the information in your credit report in order to approve a new line of credit to you. If they cannot see your report, they also cannot open the requested account.

Credit freezes do not affect your credit score in any way nor do they stop you from obtaining your free annual copy of your credit report. You are also still able to open new accounts as long as you lift the freeze temporarily which can be done at a specific time or to accommodate a request from a specific employer, company, or landlord. Unfortunately, a freeze will not stop any existing false accounts from being altered to used or fraudulent transactions from your own accounts.

Be aware that if you freeze your credit report, some people can still have access. The creditors that you already have and any debt collectors that may be acting for them as well as government agencies with probable cause can still see your report.

If you want to freeze your credit report, it is as simple as contacting each of the three major credit bureaus-Equifax, Experian, and TransUnion-supplying the necessary identifying information, and requesting the freeze. You may also need to pay a small fee which usually ranges from around $5 to $10. You will receive a confirmation in writing that will contain a PIN or password that you can use to lift the freeze after you have requested it. Ensure that you keep this documentation in a safe place as it is the only way to lift the credit freeze.

Credit freezes usually stay in place until you choose to remove or lift it but in some states, it will expire after seven years. Just like when placing the freeze, you will likely have to pay a fee which will vary from state to state.

Fraud Alerts

A fraud alert is different from a credit freeze. All a fraud alert will do is request an extra step from creditors who want to obtain a copy of your credit report. Placing a fraud alert on your credit report means that any time a creditor needs or wants to check your credit report, they will be contacting you requesting information verifying your identity and that you are indeed requesting the credit or service. Of course, this can still help prevent new lines of credit from being opened without your permission, but the process is different.

When placing a fraud alert on your credit report you are able to choose from three types of alerts. The first type is an initial fraud alert. You would use this type if you think someone may have your information but you have not had any fraudulent accounts or charges on your records yet such as in the case of a missing or stolen social security card, wallet, purse, cell phone, or mail. It will be active for 90 days.

The second type of alert is an extended fraud alert. It offers extended protection of at least seven years.

The last type of alert is called an active duty military alert. If you are in the military and want to protect your credit while deployed, you can place this alert on your report. It will last for one year and work like any other fraud alert even though you do not already have reason to believe someone has obtained your information.

Unlike credit freezes, fraud alerts are free. All you have to do is contact one of the three major credit bureaus. The one that you contact must pass the information to the other companies and it will show up on all three of your credit reports.

Chapter 8:

More Things To Know

There is already a plethora of information in the rest of this book but here in this last chapter will be some last tips and tricks to help understand and manage your credit including how to opt out of data brokers, track everything via USPS, and settle medical bills.

Opt-Out of Data Brokers

As you know, data broker or furnisher companies give consumer information to credit bureaus. All the affected agencies and other companies such as utilities that process your financial information are all considered data furnishers. They can also be stand-alone companies that work to gather information including public records. You read more about these companies in the last chapter. Now you will learn how to opt out of their lists.

This process is different for literally every company that furnishes data and can be a tedious and even annoying task. There are thousands of companies that furnish information, however, not all of them are commercial or people search companies. Most are banks and other services which cannot opt out of and will only have your information if you employ their services or open an account with them.

Take note that not all data-brokers accept opt-outs since it is not required of them. You will also likely have to submit some kind of identification to prove your identity to the company such as your driver's license. Not all companies have online forms meaning many require you to mail, fax, or call in order to opt-out. You can even pay an annual fee to a service in order to opt out of some companies without going through the trouble yourself.

Start by identifying the companies you want to opt-out of, beginning with your highest-priorities. https://www.stopdatamining.me/opt-out-list/ is a good place to start but there are also many more companies you will have to find and individually opt-out of on your own since there is no comprehensive list of data brokers available to consumers.

Group the companies that have the similar requirements. So you can take a chunk out at once. Say 10 of the companies you want to opt-out of requiring you to fax a letter and copy of your ID to them. You could print the letters and fax them all in one day. Then the next time you are free, you could call the next group, and so on until you have completed your list. You might want to save the one's you can do online until last since they will likely be the simplest. Also, be careful not to give your identifying information to any companies that seem sketchy. You should not give bad companies more information about yourself than they can achieve on their own. It is better to remain on their lists.

Another way to stop some commercial data brokers when browsing online is to download free extensions for your web browser that blocks their efforts. There are many available ??? that will stop their less-tenacious efforts that track your movements online. Try searching for extensions that block tracking and advertisements. These will prevent a lot of your information from ever making it back to data companies.

How to Use USPS Tracking Services

The United States Post Office offers services like certified mail in which you can track your mail online, by phone, or through text messaging. This is available automatically or for a fee depending on what you are mailing. Throughout this book, there have been several mentions of sending all of your official correspondence using this service. This is because it allows you to track and know when your mail has arrived as well as give you a printed receipt of when you sent the letter.

This service works because once you send a trackable item, it is labeled in a manner that allows it to be scanned at several points along its shipping route. This includes when you send it and when a delivery is made or attempted. If you want, you can also add an extra service that would require a signature from the recipient upon delivery.

To send your mail with a tracking service, you can start at the post office or online. If you go to your local post office, all you have to do is inquire about their tracking service and they will explain your options and the pricing. If you want to print your own shipping labels at home, go to the USPS.com website, create an account, and purchase postage with tracking. If you choose the online method, you will be able to print both your printing label and receipt.

Either way, you will have a receipt with a tracking number that you can use to access information about your mail. Online, visit https://tools.usps.com/go/ TrackConfirmActioninput and enter your tracking number from your receipt. To track through text messaging, send your tracking number to 28777 (2USPS). By phone, call 1-800-222-1811 at any time. The service is always available. Additionally, you can download the USPS Mobile app on your Android or iPhone. If you want automatic notifications, you can also sign up online or on the mobile application.

Using a Commercial Mail Receiving Agency

A Commercial Mail Receiving Agency (CMRA) is a service in which you can receive mail at the street address of the CMRA instead of your personal street address. This type of service is also sometimes called a mail drop. It is not like a post office box in that you can receive packages, courier packages, and other non-mail items. These services also usually give you the option of forwarding mail or holding things for pickup as well as additional services like copy, courier, and facsimile.

These services (Example: UPS Store franchises) are often of use to small business owners and international businesses. Sometimes, people use them to obtain street addresses for mail that are in a better location as well.

An often overlooked benefit to using this type of service is that you have a secured street address which you can use for credit applications, online shopping, and more, effectively protecting your personal residence from some types of fraud attempts. If you send and receive all of your important mail such as bills and statements from this type of secure mail service, you can eliminate the threat of stolen mail.

How to Settle Medical Debt

The last thing you should know about is how to settle medical debts. It is unfortunate, but in the United States, we often have to contend with high medical costs and a confusing system that can cripple us financially for years after an illness or accident. Even with insurance, there are co-pays, deductibles, and procedures that fall outside of some plans coverage. Even if you are not currently contending with medical debts, it is a good thing to understand in case they hit your family.

When you start on your journey to understand and settle your medical debts, it is important to understand that the system was not made for consumer usability. It will be a hard and tedious job that will require a lot of time, energy, and patience to complete. You will need to keep everything you receive in an organized file and pay attention to things like deadlines and necessary procedures to be successful. That being said, it can be done, even without professional help.

The worst thing you could do when faced with medical debt is ignore it, so make sure to start as soon as you are able. In most cases, you must attempt to negotiate your bills within the first 90 days of incurring the debt, otherwise, it can be sent to a collection agency, which will be explained later.

The very first thing you need to do is organize your bills. You will not receive a single bill from your hospital. You can also get billed by an ambulance company, labs, and pharmacy. Gather all of these into a file and review them to understand what you need to do. Write down the contact information for each of the services you are being billed for, what you were

177

charged for, and how much you owe for each thing. It is a good idea to put this all into a spreadsheet.

Using the information you gathered from the bills, look for billing discrepancies. If you find anything like the things listed here in your bills you can get them removed. Some things to look for are:

- Being billed for a full day's stay when you did not stay the full day such as on the day you are admitted or released

- Being billed for any items like gowns, gloves, or sheets that should be included in the price of your room

- Being billed for any medications you brought with you to the hospital

- Your insurance has not been applied to the bill if applicable

The next thing you need to do is to negotiate your bills with the original providers. You can do this once you have gotten any issues on the bills resolved, have seen how much will be paid by your insurance if you have any, and have a concrete idea of how much you can reasonably pay on the remaining balance.

Deciding how much you can pay requires you to know the final amount you are liable for, how much money you have saved, and how much money you have left over after your other bills each month. You can only skim so much to pay a new bill and you should tell your creditors this information.

Call each medical provider that you received a bill from and explain your situation and ask what they can do for you. Many times, they will be willing to settle for a smaller amount in order to get some money rather than none. If you are having trouble negotiating, there are professional medical bill negotiators that can help. Paying someone to help might be a hit to your finances in the short term but can ultimately save you thousands of dollars.

Sometimes, no matter how hard you try to prevent it, your medical bills will be sent to a collection agency. If this happens to you, there are a few things you need to know prior to working with the collection agency.

The first thing you need to know is if your bill is past the statute of limitations. The statute of limitations for medical debt can be anywhere from three to six years depending on your state and starts either the last time you made a payment or when the account became delinquent. This is important to know since it is not started on the date you received the service meaning you could have your dates off.

The statute of limitations can be restarted. A collection agency can do this by having you make a payment. Doing so will re-age the debt since the statute of limitation starts from the last payment. Then you will have to deal with the debt for another three to six years. Make sure you come to an agreement that is satisfactory to you before making payments.

Collection agencies buy debts for a fraction of what they are worth. You can use this knowledge to your advantage by offering to pay a much lower amount than you were originally billed since the collection agency will still make a profit. Ensure you are firm in the offer and obtain proof of any deal like this in writing from the agency.

Once you have settled the debt, you will receive Form 1099-C from the collection agency. This form will allow you to claim an exemption to paying the tax on the amount of the canceled debt. It is very important that you file this form with your taxes for the proper year of you can be charged taxes for money you did not have to pay.

Remember from chapter five, even settled collections will still be in your record for a long time. We are not claiming that it is an ideal situation but once you have settled your debt with the collection agency, it will not affect you as much as an open, delinquent account. It will also stop debt collection calls and letters. If possible, always go for settling debts with the condition that they delete any negative account history on you credit reports.

Credit Letters From "Hell"

Legal Disclaimer

The following letters were used personally by the author in his own disputes and battles with creditors, banks and "un-ethical" debt collection agencies.

These letters are only examples of what the author has done, and are in NO way representative of what you, the reader, can do, we do not claim that these letters will do anything for you at all. In fact, some of the letters are even borderline un-ethical. We would like the reader to know that by reading these letters they acknowledge that they are only examples of what the author has communicated to personal and commercial creditors, and are in no way suggestive of what you can do in your financial situation. The letters are also not being displayed for use as templates.

The author has been through many credit battles since his early 20's because there are so many law firms and financial companies that make tones of money just rolling right over Americans that don't have time to stand up for their rights. The stats are in their favor, who has time anyways? And who wants to pay a credit firm to do it for you, they won't put as much personal attention into the disputes as you will, most of them won't, at least.

Dispute Letter 1
Financial Companies

This letter was sent in response to a personal loan company that required the debtor to call in annually to renew their ACH information. But, the lender is supposed to remind the customer, in this example, they did not remind the customer and so a 30-day late payment was hit to his credit reports because the ACH did not renew. This was on an account that was over 10 years old with perfect credit history

XXXXXXXXXXXXXXXXXX   *CERTIFIED MAIL*

XXXXXXXXXXXXXXXXXXXX   *RETURN RECEIPT REQUESTED*

Lakewood, OH 44107

XXXXXXXXXXXXXXXXXXXXX

XXXXXXXXXXXXXXXXX

OneMain Holdings, Inc

601 N.W. Second Street

Evansville, IN 47708-1013

5-12-2018

RE: ACCOUNT # XXXXXXXXXXXXXXX /XXXX

Complaint and Demand

Hello, we would like to offer OneMain Financial the opportunity to correct a reckless and negligent malfeasance against customer (Since 2006) XXXXXXXXXXXXXXX caused by OneMain employees.

Recently we were notified that a negative missed payment was reported to all major credit bureaus against XXXXXXXX, which reduced his credit score over 200 points, originating from the OneMain account.

This account was set up in 2006 for the purpose of servicing a small balance to increase XXXXXXXXX credit score, and has been this way up to present day. You will see that the balance has always remained very low, with no interruptions. The account was set up on ACH several years ago.

Recently, the automatic ACH expired and no communication as received from OneMain to renew the ACH. Because of the expiration of the ACH, the account went into a 30 day late period, in which finally XXXXXXX was notified by OneMain, and he instructed OneMain to immediately renew the ACH in April 2018.

The customer agent XXXXXXXXX spoke with was very un-helpful regarding this situation, and stated that there was no negative credit reported since it was within 30 days. Efforts were made to explain to OneMain that the ACH error is OneMain's negligence, and that XXXXXXXXXX never received any communication to renew or remind him of the renewal of ACH.

This same customer agent (In April) assured XXXXXXX that the ACH was now renewed on the same checking account. In fact, the customer agent GUARANTEED TO XXXXXXXXXXX that the ACH was now set up with the same correct account.

Unfortunately, this agent made a mistake and set XXXXXXX up on an old expired account# number from when the account was owned by SpringLeaf.

This technical error seems highly reckless, negligent and borderline suspicious. Thus, the ACH did not go through, unbeknownst to XXXXXXX, and the delinquency continued into May, in which XXXXXXXXXX FINALLY received another call on May 10th, in which a debt collector at OneMain explained what happened, that the prior agent in April used the wrong account but there was nothing he could do about but that there is NO reason to believe that negative credit was reported.

This 2nd agent also was not very helpful with XXXXXXX and had a very dry and hostile monotone, even though XXXXXX never had the culpable mental state of defaulting, the facts are that your logistical servicing department handling ACH renewals has failed for

XXXXXXXXX, and has recklessly and negligently caused him financial harm, by reporting an INACCURATE AND UNTRUE missed payment to his credit report which declined his FICO over 100 points, we allege that you have violated many venues of the Fair Credit Acts, which brings this into the area of the Federal Question; in which case law of similar cases that have been won by the Consumer.

Any person of average intelligence would see that this account had a perfect history of payment ($25 per month for many years). We believe that because the account has been transferred to so many owners (HFC, SpringLeaf and now OneMain) that this has caused inaccurate data in your database and customer management systems.

This would also lead one to believe, based on these mistakes, that there may even be issues with your security of information. Cyber security vulnerabilities have also been proven to start with database and CRM weaknesses.

This is clearly a broad violation of Fair Credit acts.

We strongly ask that someone at OneMain investigate this case immediately, see the details for your-selves and remove the missed payment from all 3 major bureaus immediately. If this is not accommodated we have no choice but to claim our rights and allegations under

Federal Question.

By reporting false data to the major bureaus, XXXXXXXXX has lost his rights to a large private financial interest which requires an excellent credit standing to maintain. So the seriousness of our complaint and demand go well beyond this "courtesy" letter.

While you are removing the missed payment data from the credit repositories, we will need a letter from you stating that the missed payment is not accurate, that it is in the process of being deleted; for XXXXXXXXX credit responsibilities.

We will need this letter immediately emailed to Dana xxxxxxxx email(XXXXXXXXX@XXXXX.com) in letter head. Thank you for your co-operation.

Sincerely

XXXXXXXXXXXXXXXXX

XXXXXXXXXXXXXXXXXXXXXXXXXXXXXXXX

Lakewood, Ohio

XXXXXXXXXXXXXXXXXXX

XXXXXXXXXXXXXXXXX

CC: Entire corporate executive group (Left out)

XXXXXXXXX
XXXXXXXXX
XXXXXXXXXXXXXXXX
XXXXXXXXXXXXXXXXXXXX

XXXXXXXXXXXXXXXXXXX (OneMain Legal
Representative)

OneMain Holdings, Inc

601 N.W. Second Street

Evansville, IN 47708-1013

6-18-2018

RE: XXXXX, XXXXXXXX - OneMain Personal Loan
Account XXXXXXXXXXX,

This is a response to your letter dated
6/14/2018 and received via email.

ACH Expiration

OneMain did not make an appropriate
attempt to reach XXXXXXXXXX. We have no
records or voicemails of XXXXXXX
notifying XXXXXXX of the expiration of
ACH. In addition, no physical or
electronic mail was ever received from
XXXXXXX regarding this expiration.

Civil Allegations

In regards to the April 23rd, customer service phone call, XXXXXXX set time aside from his work schedule to deal with this matter when it was made aware to him that the ACH expired, upon his own discovery of course. The OneMain agent that took the call was made a critical error against XXXXXX. As stated before, the agent populated an OLD ACCCOUNT that was used under SpringLeaf, for the new 12 month ACH, so naturally this was going to return a NSF since the account was closed long ago. The glaring error here is very obvious.

XXXXXXXX was then actually contacted by a OneMain employee collector on May 10th, (unlike renewing the ACH, in which XXXXX received no such calls) and notified of the bounced payment and that the account was past due. XXXXXXXX was very confused as he was ASSURED by the agent on April 23rd that the ACH was set up again on same account it was on before expiration. This agent on May 10th stated to XXXXX that the agent on April 23rd made an error and set XXXXX up on an old bank account, so in good will he will waive the late charge and then set XXXXXXX back up on the correct active bank account.

XXXXXXX was stunned by this reckless handling of his bank account information and now suffered an automatic derogatory mark on his credit reports due to OneMain's reckless handling of his personal financial information.

Once again we are claiming that this late payment is not valid, it was caused by OneMain's error in operations.

We strongly believe we have valid case in our favor, in addition to claims for damages suffered as a result of this unfair action by OneMain.

Please respond to our original demand to the deletion of the 30-day negative payment registered now with Experian, TransUnion, Equifax and a letter stating so to XXXXX. It's our belief we are being extremely fair and generous in our demand, but if OneMain chooses to conduct such activities on its long-standing credit worthy customers with this kind of disdain or disregard, we must defend our rights and try to recover the damages caused to XXXXXX by OneMain under appropriate jurisdictions for civil matters such as these (Federal Question and Consumer Protection Acts).

Awaiting Your Response,

XXXXXXX XXXXXXXXX

Dispute Letter 2

Medical Related

This letter was used for medical bill the creditor received for items that his health insurance unjustly did not cover. So it was sent to both the hospital and the insurance company. Note, that every first letter must demand an investigation, include a Cease and Desist clause, sent via USPS certified mail and have a 30 day response deadline.

This particular letter is the second one after all these demands were made.

Do not use emotions in letters, strictly state the facts in a chain of events like a police report, allude to the laws in place and then make your demands professionally and cordially, but in a manner that denotes you mean business and will not stop.

XXXX XXXXX

XXXXXXXXXX   XXXXXXXXX

Scottsdale, AZ

XXXXXXXXXXXXXXXXXX

MetroHealth System

Billing Disputes

PO Box 931703

Cleveland, OH 44193

12-2-2017

RE: acct: record# xxxxxxx amount $629.01

Dispute

Hello - this is our second attempt to contact you. Our first attempt was a certified letter mailed to the address provided on the letter head of the billing statement we retrieved at an invalid address.

We are disputing the validity of this debt and are claiming alleged violations of the Fair Credit Acts.

More specifically:

- The date and time of the billing origination and distribution.

-

- Insurance payment/non-payment discrepancies.

-

- Invalid billing addresses and contact names

We are requesting that you stop all collection and credit reporting activity, until this dispute is resolved. Thank you

Credit Letter 3

Medical Collections Vendor

Many medical company debt collectors need to be extra careful they don't violate Fair Credit Acts, so generally getting them to respond or dropping your file is very common.

XXXXXXXXXXXXX

XXXXXXXXXXXXXXXXXXXXXXXXXXXXX

Scottsdale, AZ 85251

Xxxxxxxxxxxxxxx

xxxxxxxxxxx

xxxxxxxxxxxxxxxxx, corporate rep.

XXXXXXXXXXXXXXXXXXXXXXXXXXX

3250 W. Market Street

Suite 1

Fairlawn, OH 44333

Also sent via email @
xxxxxxxxxxxxxxxxxxxx
xxxxxxxxxxxxxxxxxxxxxxxxx
xxxxxxxxxxxxxxxxxxxxxxxxxxxxx

12-5-2017

Dispute

Hello – this is our third attempt to contact you. Our first attempt was a certified letter- mailed to the address provided on the letter head of the copied letter attached to our letter. Our second letter was send via USPS certified, of which they were bounced and the Emails were returned un-deliverable.

We are disputing the validity of this debt and are claiming alleged violations of the Fair Credit Acts.

We are requesting that you stop all collection and credit reporting activity, as we did in the letter dated for 11/27/2017, in which we included a copy of the certified receipt in the letter, until this can be resolved.

Thank you, xxxxxxxxxxxxxxx, et al.

CC: CCF

Credit Inquiry Dispute Process

Trying to get legitimate inquiries deleted can be difficult, however, if an auto loan or mortgage company "shot-gunned" your credit request to multiple wholesale lenders, who all have to check your credit once, then you can end up with 5-10 hard inquiries on your report that will most assuredly reduce your FICO significantly.

The startling stat is that most lenders you are negotiating with will actually tell you not to worry because it is a "SOFT" credit hit....or that your score won't suffer that much because the Credit Bureaus' algorithm takes this into consideration and knows that you are shopping for a loan within a short window of time

Don't go for it, make sure they know that you are only allowing one credit check If they don't do this, then you have easy case in deletion of the credit inquiries they originated on you.

Sending in an inquiry dispute needs to go to both the credit bureau and the creditor that made the inquiry. Very few creditors do this! You will assuredly piss people off, but do not back down. They will get pissed off because they know the fines and penalties for violating Fair Credit Acts and/or Consumer Acts are severe and long-lasting as far as publicity goes.

<u>Real Credit Dispute</u>

EXPERIAN
PO BOX 9556
ALLEN, TX 75013

THIS IS A CREDIT INQUIRY DISPUTE ORIGINATED BY
XXXXXXXXXXXXXXX

<u>ENCLOSURES</u>

- DISPUTE LETTER AND IDENTIFICATION
INFORMATION

- CREDIT INQUIRY DISPUTES.

- COPY OF SS CARD

- COPY OF DRIVERS LICENSE

- COPY OF INSURANCE BILL

- COPY OF UTILITY BILL

- FEDERAL COMPLAINT

TRANSUNION CUSTOMER RELATIONS

PO BOX 1000

CHESTER, PA 19022

THIS IS A CREDIT DISPUTE ORIGINATED BY
XXXXXXXXXXXXXXXXXXX

ENCLOSURES

- DISPUTE LETTER

- CREDIT INQUIRY DISPUTES.

- COPY OF SS CARD

- COPY OF DIVERS LICENSE

- COPY OF INSURANCE BILL

- COPY OF UTILITY BILL

- FEDERAL COMPLAINT

EQUIFAX INFOMRATION SERVICES
PO BOX 740256
ATLANTA, GA 30374

THIS IS A CREDIT DISPUTE ORIGINATED BY
XXXXXXXXXXXXXXXXXX

ENCLOSURES

- DISPUTE LETTER

- CREDIT INQUIRY DISPUTES.

- COPY OF SS CARD

- COPY OF DIVERS LICENSE

- COPY OF INSURANCE BILL

- COPY OF UTILITY BILL

- FEDERAL COMPLAINT

XXXXXXXXXXX
XXXXXXXXXXXXXXXXXXXXXXXX
Phoenix, AZ 85048
XXXXXXXXXXXXXXXXXXXXX

JANUARY 19, 2011

Dear Experian:

THIS IS A CREDIT INQUIRY DISPUTE

THE FOLLOWING CREDIT INQUIRIES ARE NOT MINE, NOR DID I EVER AUTHORIZE THESE COMPANIES TO CHECK MY CREDIT VERBALLY OR CONTRACTUALLY. I NEVER GAVE THE BELOW-DESCRIBED COMPANIES THAT CONDUCTED THE INQUIRIES PERMISSION TO DO BUSINESS WITH ME.

REPORTING INACCURATE INFORMATION ON MY CREDIT FILE IS A VIOLATION OF THE FAIR CREDIT ACTS. YOU ARE REQUIRED BY LAW TO INVESTIGATE THOUROUGHLY AND CONFIRM.

RECORDS INDICATE THERE WAS A CONSIDERABLE NEGLIGENCE IN THE INVESTIGATION OF XXXXXXXXXXX PREVIOUS CREDIT INQUIRY DISPUTES. BECAUSE OF THIS AND EXPERIAN'S LACK OF CONCERN REGARDING XXXX XXXXXXXX CREDIT REPORTING ACTIVITIES, A FEDERAL COMPLAINT IS BEING FILED WITH THE ARIZONA U.S. DISTRICT COURT FOR FAIR CREDIT ACT VIOLATIONS AND DAMAGES AGAINST EXPERIAN FOR FAILURE TO RESOLVE THESE DISPUTES.

PLEASE DELETE THE LISTED INQUIRIES IN DISPUTE AS SOON AS POSSIBLE.

Sincerely,
XXXXXXXXXXXXXXXXXXX

Inquiries in dispute:

CREDIT UNION WEST

Address:
PO BOX 38300
PHOENIX AZ 85069
No phone number available
Date of Request:
10/21/2010
Address Identification Number:
Not Available

CREDCO

Address:
12395 FIRST AMERICAN WAY
POWAY CA 92064
No phone number available
Date of Request:
10/19/2010
Address Identification Number:
Not Available

US BANK

Address:
180 5TH ST E
SAINT PAUL MN 55101
No phone number available
Date of Request:
03/03/2010
Address Identification Number:
Not Available

CREDSTAR

Address:
6350 LAUREL CANYON BLVD FL 4
NORTH HOLLYWOOD CA 91606
No phone number available
Date of Request:
06/30/2009
Address Identification Number:

CREDIT PLUS

Address:
31550 WINTERPLACE PKWY
SALISBURY MD 21804
No phone number available
Date of Request:
05/21/2009
Address Identification Number:

WELLS FARGO BANK

Address:
PO BOX 5445
PORTLAND OR 97228
(877) 778-5697
Date of Request:
01/15/2009
Address Identification Number:

XXXXXXXXXXXXXXXXXX
XXXXXXXXXXXXXXXXXXXXXXXXXXXXXXXXXXX
Phoenix, AZ 85048
XXXXXXXXXXXXXXXXXXXX

JANUARY 19, 2011

Dear TRANSUNION:

THIS IS A CREDIT INQUIRY DISPUTE

THE FOLLOWING CREDIT INQUIRIES ARE NOT MINE, NOR DID I EVER AUTHORIZE THESE COMPANIES TO CHECK MY CREDIT VERBALLY OR CONTRACTUALLY. I NEVER GAVE THE BELOW-DESCRIBED COMPANIES THAT CONDUCTED THE INQUIRIES PERMISSION TO DO BUSINESS WITH ME.

REPORTING INACCURATE INFORMATION ON MY CREDIT FILE IS A VIOLATION OF THE FAIR CREDIT ACTS. YOU ARE REQUIRED BY LAW TO INVESTIGATE THOUROUGHLY AND CONFIRM.

RECORDS INDICATE THERE WAS A CONSIDERABLE NEGLIGENCE IN THE INVESTIGATION OF XXXXXX XXXXXXXXXXX PREVIOUS CREDIT INQUIRY DISPUTES. BECAUSE OF THIS AND TRANSUNION'S LACK OF CONCERN REGARDING XXXXXXXXXXXXXXXX CREDIT REPORTING ACTIVITIES, A FEDERAL COMPLAINT IS BEING FILED WITH THE ARIZONA U.S. DISTRICT COURT FOR FAIR CREDIT ACT VIOLATIONS AND DAMAGES AGAINST TRANSUNION FOR FAILURE TO RESOLVE THESE DISPUTES.

PLEASE DELETE THE LISTED INQUIRIES IN DISPUTE AS SOON AS POSSIBLE.

Sincerely,
XXXXXXXXXXXXXXXXXXXXXXXX

Inquiries in dispute:

CREATIVE LENDING SOL via CREDSTAR

6350 LAUREL CANYON

4TH FLR SUITE 450

NORTH HOLLYWOO , CA 91606

(818) 762-6262

Requested On:

Inquiry Type:

06/30/2009

Individual

JOE KLEIN ENTERPRISE via CREDIT PLUS

530 RIVERSIDE DR

SALISBURY , MD 21801

(410) 742-9551

Requested On:

Inquiry Type:

05/21/2009

Individual

XXXXXXXXXXXXXX
XXXXXXXXXXXXXXXXXXXXXXXXXXXXXXXXXXXX
Phoenix, AZ 85048
XXXXXXXXXXXXXXXXXXXXXXX

JANUARY 19, 2011

Dear EQUIFAX:

THIS IS A CREDIT INQUIRY DISPUTE

THE FOLLOWING CREDIT INQUIRIES ARE NOT MINE, NOR DID I EVER AUTHORIZE THESE COMPANIES TO CHECK MY CREDIT VERBALLY OR CONTRACTUALLY. I NEVER GAVE THE BELOW-DESCRIBED COMPANIES THAT CONDUCTED THE INQUIRIES PERMISSION TO DO BUSINESS WITH ME.

REPORTING INACCURATE INFORMATION ON MY CREDIT FILE IS A VIOLATION OF THE FAIR CREDIT ACTS. YOU ARE REQUIRED BY LAW TO INVESTIGATE THOUROUGHLY AND CONFIRM.

RECORDS INDICATE THERE WAS A CONSIDERABLE NEGLIGENCE IN THE INVESTIGATION OF XXXXXXXXXXXXXX XXXXX PREVIOUS CREDIT INQUIRY DISPUTES. BECAUSE OF THIS AND EQUIFAX'S LACK OF CONCERN REGARDING XXXXXXXXXXXXXXXXXXXX CREDIT REPORTING ACTIVITIES, A FEDERAL COMPLAINT IS BEING FILED WITH THE ARIZONA U.S. DISTRICT COURT FOR FAIR CREDIT ACT VIOLATIONS AND DAMAGES AGAINST EQUIFAX FOR FAILURE TO RESOLVE THESE DISPUTES.

PLEASE DELETE THE LISTED INQUIRIES IN DISPUTE AS SOON AS POSSIBLE.

Sincerely,

XXXXX XXXXXXXXXXXX

203

Inquiries in dispute:

CITIBANK USA, NA 04/15/10
CITIBANK USA, NA
2195 University Park Blvd
Layton, UT 840411263

COX COMMUNICATIONS 11/05/09
COX COMMUNICATIONS
17602 N Black Canyon Hwy
Phoenix, AZ 850531936

CHASE CREDIT
RESEARCH, INC

06/30/09
CHASE CREDIT RESEARCH, INC.
6350 Laurel Canyon Blvd 4th Fl
North Hollywood, CA 916063200

CHASE CREDIT
RESEARCH, INC.
…
06/30/09
CHASE CREDIT RESEARCH, INC.
6350 Laurel Canyon Blvd 4th Fl
North Hollywood, CA 916063200

CREDIT BUREAU OF
DELMARVA …1518609740
05/21/09

CREDIT BUREAU OF DELMARVA
530 Riverside Dr
Salisbury, MD 218016402

Negative Delinquent Account / Collections Account Dispute Letter

This letter was issued for a ISP account that billed the creditor at an old address. The creditor has moved out of state and opened up a new account with the same ISP. His dispute was that the ISP's internal databases should all be synchronized and know that he has a new account and to have sent him the old account balance to the new residence in a new state. Like most other letters, this negative account was deleted by the Major Credit Bureaus immediately.

Xxxxxx xxxxxxxx
xxxxxxxxxxxxxxxxxxxxxxxxxxx
Scottsdale, AZ 85251
xxxxxxxxxxxxxxxxxxxxxxxxx
xxxxxxxxxxxxxxxxxxxxxxxxx

(A COLLECTIONS VENDOR FOR A MAJOR INTERNET SERICE PROVIDER)
XXXXXXXXXXXXXXXX XXXX,XXXXXXXXXX
DALLAS, TX 75240

6-18-2018

RE: xxxxxxxxxxxxxxx / (A major ISP account)-xxxxxxxxxxxxx

Dispute, Demand and Violation

This claim for debt is now in dispute and pre-litigation. Please see our claim below.

The amount of $53.09 was brought to our attention by a negative credit reporting rating to xxxxxxxxxx credit reports.

This debt is not known or recognized by xxxxxxxxxx. xxxxxxxxxxx last [ISP] account was located at XXXXXXXXXXX Street and was paid and closed In full and the one before that in XXXXXXXXXX was also paid and closed in January of this year.

If there were any other outstanding balances, they would have been included in the final statement under XXXXXXXXX, XXXXXXX at his last [ISP] address of XXXXXXXXXX Street or the mailing address that was in that account.

[ISP] and its contracted collection company are in gross violation of the Fair Debt Collection acts, specifically, it is your job to update your database of new billing addresses and notify the account holder of the balance owned.

XXXXXXXXXXX made it very clear to [ISP] that his new address was located at XXXXXXXXXXX Street (Service location) since they obviously set up an account for him there too, it IS [ISP] responsibility to forward billing statements to the appropriate addresses.

XXXXXXXXXXX is claiming his rights under the Fair Credit Acts and are demanding that COX and its collection entity DELETE the negative credit rating you have reported to the 3 major credit bureaus immediately and any other repositories.

We expect a response within 15 business days of this letter or sooner.

Regards,

XXXXXXXXX XXXXXXXXXXXX

CC: [ISP] Legal Dept. / EXPERIAN / TRANSUNION / EQUIFAX.
CC: COLLECTIONS COMPANY VENDOR
CC: Texas State Attorney General Office

XXXXXXXX
XXXXXXXXXXXX
SCOTTSDALE, AZ 85251
XXXXXXXXXXXXXXXXXXXX

EXPERIAN
475 ANTON BLVD
COSTA MESA, CA 92626
ATTN: LEGAL DEPARTMENT

6-18-2018

RE: RE:XXXXXXXXXXX / ACCOUNT [ISP]-
XXXXXXXXXXXXX

(There are attachments)

Attached is a pre-litigation complaint
and demand to a collection company that [ISP]
retains for unpaid debts.

Our dispute and claim is that this debt
was never brought to our attention, if it is
even valid, and they never made any attempt to
update their billing address even though the
defendant XXXXXXXX had an active RESIDENTIAL
account with [ISP] when these alleged claims
for debts were made earlier this year at an
old address. IN ADDITION, THE LAST ACCOUNT
XXXXXX had in XXXXXXXXX was closed and paid
over the phone with a customer service
representative in February of this year, so we
do not even recognize or agree with the debt
claim.

THIS IS in dispute and we are preparing a possible claim under Federal Question jurisdiction and the Consumer Protection Acts.

We are asking you to investigate this matter and see the error for yourself and then delete the illegal negative credit rating that [ISP] and its credit collection entity has illegally reported to you. XXXXXXXXX does have claims for damages he is prepared to defend and pursue if needed.

Thank you for your co-operation in this matter.

Sincerely,

XXXXXXXXXXXXXXXXX

XXXXXXXXX
XXXXXXXXXXXXXXXXXXXXXXX
SCOTTSDALE, AZ 85251
XXXXXXXXXXXXXXXXXXXXXXXXX
XXXXXXXXXXXXXXXX

EQUIFAX
1550 PEACHTREE STREET, N.M.
ATLANTA, GEORGIA 30309
ATTN: LEGAL DEPARTMENT

6-18-2018

RE: RE: XXXXXXXXXXXXX / ACCOUNT [ISP ACCOUNT#]

(There are attachments)

Attached is a pre-litigation complaint and demand to a collection company that {ISP} retains for unpaid debts.

Our dispute and claim is that this debt was never brought to our attention, if it is even valid, and they never made any attempt to update their billing address even though the defendant XXXXXXXXXXX had an active RESIDENTIAL account with [ISP] when these alleged claims for debts were made earlier this year at an old address. IN ADDITION, THE LAST ACCOUNT XXXXXXXXXXXXX had in XXXX was closed and paid over the phone with a customer service representative in February of this year, so we do not even recognize or agree with the debt claim.

THIS IS in dispute and we are preparing a possible claim under Federal Question jurisdiction and the Consumer Protection Acts.

We are asking you to investigate this matter and see the error for yourself and then delete the illegal negative credit rating that [ISP] and its credit collection entity has illegally reported to you. XXXXXXXXXX does have claims for damages he is prepared to defend and pursue if needed.

Thank you for your co-operation in this matter.

Sincerely,

XXXXXXX XXXXXXXXXX

XXXXXXXXX
XXXXXXXXXXXXXXXXXXXXXXXXXXX
SCOTTSDALE, AZ 85251
XXXXXXXXXXXXXXXXXXXXXXXXXXX
XXXXXXXXXXXXXXXXX

TRANSUNION
555 WEST ADAMS STREET
CHICAGO, IL 60661
ATTN: LEGAL DEPARTMENT

6-18-2018

(There are attachments)

RE: RE: XXXXXXXXXXXXXXX / ACCOUNT [ISP ACCT #]

(There are attachments)

Attached is a pre-litigation complaint and demand to a collection company that [ISP] retains for unpaid debts.

Our dispute and claim is that this debt was never brought to our attention, if it is even valid, and they never made any attempt to update their billing address even though the defendant XXXXXXX had an active RESIDENTIAL account with [ISP] when these alleged claims for debts were made earlier this year at an old address. IN ADDITION, THE LAST ACCOUNT XXXXXXX had in XXXXX was closed and paid over the phone with a customer service representative in February of this year, so we do not even recognize or agree with the debt claim.

THIS IS in dispute and we are preparing a possible claim under Federal Question jurisdiction and the Consumer Protection Acts.

We are asking you to investigate this matter and see the error for yourself and then delete the illegal negative credit rating that [ISP] and its credit collection entity has illegally reported to you. XXXXXXXXXXXXX does have claims for damages he is prepared to defend and pursue if needed.

Thank you for your co-operation in this matter.

Sincerely,

XXXXXXXXXXXXXXXXXXXXXXXXX

IDENTIFICATION

CURRENT ADDRESS:

XXXXXXXXXXXXXXXXX
XXXXXXXXXXXXXXXXXX
XXXXXXXXXXXXXXXXXXXX

SSN#:

XXX-XX-XXXX

DOB:

XX-XX-XXXX

CREDITOR MAKING REPORTING ACTIVITY:

ISP COMPANY AND IT'S COLLECTIONS VENDOR

REASON FOR DISPUTE:

DEBT NOT VALID AND FCRA VIOLATION

XXXXXXXXXXXXX
XXXXXXXXXXXXXXXXXXXXXXXXXXXXXXXXXXXX
MENTOR, OHIO 44060
(216)XXX-XXXX
XXXXX@XXX.COM

XXXXXXXXXXXXXXXXXXXXXXXXX
XXXXXXXXXXXXXXXXXXX
CARROLLTON, TX 75007-1958
XXXXXXXXXXXXXXXXXXXXXX

RE: XXXXXXXXXXXXXXXX
XXXXXXXXXXXXXXXX
XXXXXXXXXXXXXXX
CREDITOR: XXXXXXXXXXXX
XXXX ACCT#: XXXXXXXXXXXX
XXXXXXXXXXXXXXXXXXXXXXXXXXX
AMOUNT: $230.36

NOVEMBER 13, 2017

CEASE AND DESIST

This letter is a dispute and complaint against XXXXXXXXXXXXX, IT'S ASSOCIATED ENTITIES and XXXXXXXXXXXXXXXX, LP. for the above account information and dollar amount that they are requesting from XXXXXXXXXXXXXXXX.

To be more clear, THIS ACCOUNT IS IN DISPUTE. Please suspend all collection and credit reporting activity until this has been resolved.

This account is also in pre-litigation for possible fraud and violations of the Fair Credit Acts. Please forward any documents or evidence you have showing proof of XXXXXXXXXXXXX having service with XXXXX and how he was specifically charged for $230.36 in exact detail to the

215

address listed on the letterhead.

Briefly, XXXXXXXXXXXXX claims that the service promised by XXXXXX customer service in July of 2017 was not actually available in his residence; however, when service was installed, only phone service was on, and it was later explained to XXXXXXXXXXXXX by XXXXX Corporate that that was the only service available at his residence.

XXXXXXXXXXXXX claims he never used the phone service, and he was led to believe that he was getting the "XXXXXXXXXXXXX BUNDLE", which was a total deception by XXXXXX. Thus, XXXXXXXXXXXXX canceled the service without using it, feeling deceived and swindled by XXXXXXXXX for set-up charges and deposits.

Regards,

XXXXXXXX XXXXXXXXXXXXXXXXXX

CC: CORPORATE HEADQUARTERS

LEGAL DEPT / GENERAL COUNSEL

XXXXXXXXXXX
Dallas, TX 75202

CC: CT CORPORATION SYSTEM (STATUTORY AGENT)

CC: CT CORPORATION SYSTEM (STATUTORY AGENT)

CC: OHIO STATE ATTORNEY GENERAL

Unfortunately my legal advisor stated that I cannot place anymore of the real heavy hitters in this book. However, stay tuned because we are working on publishing them so that they meet all legal requirements, including a real Federal case we filed (pro se) against a credit card company that worked gloriously and cost under $100.

But remember this one thing, letters sent to the RIGHT people GET ATTENTION, period, especially now in today's digital world where most messages are emails or texts and area never read.

Made in the USA
Columbia, SC
24 August 2019